M000315855

The Essentials of
CAVE DIVING
Third Edition

Jill Heinerth

Published by:

Heinerth Productions Inc.

High Springs, Florida USA

First published 2010, Rev. 3.0 – February 2017

Copyright © Jill Heinerth

Photography, illustrations and text

By Jill Heinerth

All rights reserved. No part of this book may be reproduced in any form or by any electronic or mechanical means, or stored in any retrieval system, or transmitted in any form by any means, electronic, mechanical, photocopying, recording or otherwise, without permission of the publisher. All registered trademarks acknowledged.

This manual is not intended to be used as a substitute for proper dive training. Cave diving is a dangerous sport and training should only be conducted under the safe supervision of an active cave diving instructor until you are fully qualified and then only in conditions and circumstances which are as good or better than the conditions in which you were trained. Careful risk assessment, continuing education and skills practice may lessen your likelihood of an accident but are never a guarantee for complete safety.

This book assumes a basic knowledge of diving technique and should be used to complement a training course specializing in cave diving techniques.

Cover Photo: Tom Morris and Dr. Kenny Broad explore an area called the Crystal Palace in Abaco, Bahamas.

Book design Heinerth Productions Inc.

www.IntoThePlanet.com

Printed in the USA

ISBN 978-1-940944-24-1

Available on the author's website and Amazon worldwide.

Acknowledgments--------------------------------

In a project of this magnitude, there are many people who deserve thanks. I am truly grateful for the opportunities afforded to me by my parents, who bought me LEGO instead of Barbies and invested in a canoe that we still use. We went camping and hiking instead of driving to Disney and struck the word "impossible" from our vocabulary.

Paul Heinerth deserves the utmost respect for steering me into the cave safely when I was content to explore without proper guidance. I owe the late Wes Skiles a debt of gratitude for helping me find the fit between my creativity and obsession for the underwater world. And to Jim Bowden, the sincerest thanks for the constant encouragement to explore, write and follow my passion without limitations.

I owe a great debt to the many friends and colleagues that lost their lives, but illustrated a safer path for all of us to follow. They will be sadly missed and always remembered for their contributions and dedication to the sport.

I also want to thank the multitude of dive partners, expeditionary colleagues and dear friends whose faces either fill this text or simply overwhelm my brain with memorable experiences: Barbara am Ende, Robert Bradish, Kenny Broad, John Buxton, Kathleen Byers, Ron Carmichael, Linda Claridge, Christian Clark, Cas Dobbin, Bev and Trey Clanton, Jacki Clark, Joel Clark, Michael Costales, Rich Courtney, Klaus Christiansen, Garry Dallas, Richard Dreher, Joe Dituri, Jeff Dodd, Susan Eaton, Peter Eklund, Ali Falcone, John Falcone, Helen Farr, Martyn Farr, Amy Ferguson, Michel Angelo Gagliardi, Mark Goodman, Brett Gonzalez, Drazen Goricki, Dmitri Gorski, Debra Green, Larry Green, Kevin Gurr, Hugh Hansard, Jónína Herdís Ólafsdóttir, Lamar Hires, Tom Iliffe, Danny Jetmore, Kelly Jessop, Brian Kakuk, Wayne Kinard, Klaus Kristiansen, Bruno Kuzamanic, Marc Laukien, Marissa Lasso, Rasmus Lauritsen, Steve Lewis, Annette Long, Graham Maddocks, Mark Long, Etienne Mackenson, Matt Matthes, Geoffrey May, Mark Meadows, Cory Mearns, Tom Morris, Kristine Rae Olmsted, John Olivero, Rick Palm, Brian Pease, Renée Power, Nissa Quanstrom, Rich Rosato, Wendy Quimby, Jason Sapp, John Sapp, Dave Sawatzky, Becky Kagan Schott, Phil Short, Mary Sloan, Kim Smith, Gemma Smith, Daphne Soares, Eric Stadtmueller, Rick Stanley, Bill Stone, Trisha Stovel, Terry Thomas, Paul Toomer, Joel Tower, John Vanderleest, Matt Vinzant, Craig Walters, John Weisbrich, Mark Wenner, Pam Wooten, Michael Wright, Edmund Yiu and Khrista Zand. I also wish to thank Nic Alvarado, Richard Nordstrom, Georgia Shemitz, Gene Page, SednaEpic.com and Pam Wooten for additional photos. Dive Rite, Halcyon, Light & Motion, Suunto, Apeks and OMS provided equipment photography.

Dr. Neil Pollock is owed special thanks for assistance with improving the glossary at the end of the book. Stefanie Martina deserves special thanks for her research support on the article about IPE.

Staying on top of the diving game can be financially challenging. Many sponsors have supported me through creative collaborations that allow us to swap services and goods. Others have outright gifted me with merchandise that would have been difficult for me to afford. Many manufacturers also gave me the opportunity to stay on the cutting edge while I tested and previewed things that were not yet on the market. To those companies I am grateful. Their support and kindness is always appreciated. Suunto and Aquatica have gone beyond all others in their generosity and support and Santi has not only kept me dry but also supported causes that are important to me. Light & Motion, Hollis, Kühl, Aqualung, Apeks, PSI, Custom Divers, Fourth Element, PMI Rope, Waterproof, Halcyon, Bare and others have offered excellent tools for my work. It is a small industry we work in, but these and other manufacturers have big hearts. Thanks also to the manufacturers who listen to my pleas for women-specific gear and try their best to make it happen.

Most importantly, I wish to express the deepest gratitude to my loving husband Robert McClellan, who supports me in every aspect of my life and career. It can't be easy being married to a girl who runs off each day to partake in one of the most dangerous sports ever conceived. His patience, love and guidance continue to lift me to greater heights. His tireless efforts to edit, market and ship books to the post office on his bicycle, allow us to continue writing new manuals and participate in an enviable life. I could ask for nothing more!

Jill Heinerth---

Explorer in Residence, Royal Canadian Geographical Society

More people have walked on the moon, than have been to some of the places that Jill's exploration has taken her right here on the earth. From dangerous technical dives deep inside underwater caves to searching for new ecosystems inside giant Antarctic icebergs, to the lawless desert border area between Egypt and Libya while a civil war raged around her, Jill's curiosity and passion about our watery planet is the driving force in her life.

In recognition of her lifetime achievement, Jill was awarded the inaugural *Medal for Exploration*. Established by the *Royal Canadian Geographical Society*, the medal recognizes singular achievements and the pursuit of excellence by an outstanding Canadian explorer. Jill is a Fellow of the *Explorers Club* and a member of the inaugural class of the *Women Diver's Hall of Fame*. She received the *Wyland ICON Award,* an honor she shares with several of her underwater heroes including Jacques Cousteau, Robert Ballard and Dr. Sylvia Earle and is the recipient of the diving community's most prestigious award, the NOGI, from the *Academy of Underwater Arts and Sciences*. She was named a *Living Legend* by *Sport Diver Magazine* and selected as *Scuba Diving Magazine's - Sea Hero of the Year.*

Jill's photography and writing have been featured in prominent publications and major media outlets around the world. She regularly contributes to the development of training materials for international dive organizations, and is the author of numerous books on cave diving and underwater photography.

With her creative collaborator, the late Wes Skiles, Jill wrote, produced, and appeared in numerous underwater adventure films and television programs, including the award winning PBS documentary series *Water's Journey*. She has been called upon by Hollywood producers as a diving technical consultant and camera operator and produces independent film projects through her company Heinerth Productions Inc.

With the *We Are Water Project,* she has produced a documentary film, book, live presentation and interactive web resources to help steer an educational effort for everyday behavioral changes that will lead to greater access to and preservation of our endangered fresh water resources. In support of this effort,

Jill and husband Robert McClellan rode their bicycles 4,300 miles across Canada, from British Columbia to Newfoundland in 2013, meeting people and through presentations to groups large and small, spread the message of "water literacy." Her website *www.IntoThePlanet.com* provides links to her exploration and water advocacy efforts.

CAVE DIVING
TODAY

CHAPTER

Cave Diving Today----------------------------------

Introduction abridged from the Original Edition

A pockmarked, turquoise van hobbles over the dirt road throwing up a film of limestone dust, making the pines look like Christmas trees. 27-year old Agnes Milowka is relieved to stop, since the clanging tanks and shifting equipment have been ringing in her ears for what seems an eternity. She heaves the cumbersome side door open to reveal a mountain of gear; tanks on top of scooters on top of yesterday's take-out and next week's laundry. She's been making this drive every night after work for months, punching the clock at Dive Rite, dealing with life's necessities and then hitting the spring for a solitary swim through cathedrals of rock. Often surfacing well after midnight, she packs up the van and does it all again the following day. She both fascinates and frightens cave diving pioneers like Wes Skiles who discloses, "She reminds me of myself."

A team enters the cave at Orange Grove Sink at Wes Skiles Peacock Springs State Park. Photo: Jill Heinerth

Skiles recalls his earliest forays in cave diving, when he strung countless spools of braided line through boundless empty caverns. In 1970, world record cave penetrations peaked just over 2,000 feet. Within the decade the record eclipsed 5,000 feet. As underground secrets were brought into the light, diving teams like Skiles' "Mole Tribe" were charting hundreds of thousands of feet of passages in dozens of new caves deep under Florida. Air bottom times followed by air decompression led to long, painful nights and eventual trips to hyperbaric chambers in Gainesville and Tallahassee. The Tribe paid dearly with their bodies, and friends lost in the murky depths. Their efforts were both celebrated and condemned. In the very dawn of the sport, there were attempts by Florida legislators to ban cave diving completely. Locals were tired of seeing the hangtag, warning signs, indicating how many divers had lost their lives at a particular spring that year.

More than forty years later, the sport of cave diving has changed dramatically. On an attempt to check off the last corner of the map of Ginnie Springs, Agnes Milowka recalled, "suddenly and unexpectedly, I found myself at the end of the line… with a bunch of gas… and thought, now what do I do?" Over 4,500 feet back, while following exploration lines placed by James Toland and Andrew Ainslie, she realized that all she had was a small safety spool carrying a meager 125 feet of line. Chuckling to herself, she carefully uncoiled the line and launched her exploration career. "I'd be lying if I said I didn't get a kick out of this, but, I am under no illusions. In the scheme of things, my little sojourn 100 feet into new passage means absolutely nothing. It's not a cure for cancer. It's not even a footnote to the exploration that has been done and is being done around cave country, not to mention the world." What is does illustrate is a brave new paradigm in cave diving.

Warning signs placed at the entrance to popular caves have aided in preventing deaths of unqualified divers. Photo: Jill Heinerth

With old records shattered almost daily, it is hard to imagine that accidents are declining in cave diving. Thirty years ago, bodies of ill-equipped, open water instructors were dragged hundreds of feet out of darkened passages. Now it is rare to find unqualified divers in the depths of Florida's systems. Instead, a trend towards long-range recoveries is developing. Divers moving recklessly, beyond their skill and experience, are adding tasks that eclipse their ability and control. A typical recovery these days requires a team of scooter driving, rebreather divers with multiple bailout bottles and substantial surface support.

Perhaps the most significant technical innovation in cave diving over the last decade has been the proliferation of rebreathers. In fact, closed circuit rebreathers (CCRs) were employed long before traditional SCUBA in caves of the United Kingdom. In 1945, Graham Balcombe began exploration of Keld Head by walking finless on the bottom while breathing from a military surplus rebreather. Further efforts by Balcombe, John Buxton and others, yielded significant discoveries in the famed Wookey Hole and other sites.

Rebreathers are now ubiquitous in cave diving. Photo: Jill Heinerth

The combination of rebreathers with DPVs has allowed for significant increases in traffic at cave landmarks such as the Henkel Restriction of Ginnie Springs. What was recently out of range of most divers is now a regular dive for relative novices with money to spare for technology and toys. The cave zones that were restricted to divers using stage bottles and/or scooters can now be accessed by CCR cave divers with time on their hands.

The earliest cave divers employed sidemount diving methods; carrying their cylinders on their sides, below their armpits. This streamlined technique somehow fell into obscurity in the United States. Instead, Canadian diver, Dr. George Benjamin, developed a manifold system that linked tanks together. Sidemount equipment became restricted to the domain of small passages, and the tool of divers who were willing to sew their own custom harnesses. Now the availability of equipment has spawned a renaissance in this technique.

Cave diving lights are upgrading faster than cameras and PCs these days. Gone are the days of sealed-lead-acid monstrosities that required butt-mounting to be swimmable. Today's back-up lights are brighter than our best primary lights of just ten years ago. Nickel Metal Hydride, Lithium Ion and Lithium Polymer batteries have lengthened burn times. HID and LED bulbs have increased power and duration. Recent advances in semiconductors, coupled with improved controllers and dimmers add to time underwater. Amateur videographers and their buddies now carry 200-watt lamps, producing 16,000 lumens, previously found only on Hollywood movie sets.

Todays cave divers wear personal computers that exceed the capabilities found on early space shots. A better understanding of mathematical algorithms and decompression have fostered development of new deco models. The modern cave diver has an understanding of various mathematical blueprints and how they affect the human body. They plan personal Gradient Factors, use exotic gases, and crunch profiles on their laptops.

Modern DPVs have been juiced up with new battery technologies that increase the diver's range to staggering limits. Reliability and availability have increased, resulting in intensified traffic in caves. But, with inexperienced scooter drivers, comes damage to fragile geology. As a result, most state parks in Florida have banned the use of scooters inside their caves. Wes Skiles is worried about the damage and about cave divers going too far, too fast. After learning of traffic damage at the remote Henkel Restriction in the Devil's System, he remarked in early 2010, "…if you haven't swam to the Henkel, you shouldn't be at the Henkel." DPVs are no replacement for serially learning a cave.

Few cave divers today realize that Florida's, Devil's Ear cave system was once colored completely black. Years of traffic, bubbles and pulling have resulted in the loss of the geothite covering on the underwater surfaces. Worse yet, scooters and poor buoyancy have left rifts and gouges in the bottom sediments. Delicate speleothems in Mexico's cenotes have been thoughtlessly destroyed and passively eroded by bubbles. Other systems, such as Cow Springs and Troy Springs, have been the victims of vandalism; divers carving their initials in clay banks and soft limestone for the sake of posterity.

Advances in technical diving lights and wrist-mounted computers have revolutionized cave diving in the last two decades. Photo: Jill Heinerth

Cave diving instructor Pam Wooten enters the cave at Devil's Eye, part of the very popular system at Ginnie Springs in Florida. Photo: Jill Heinerth

In the least ten years, cave maps that were closely held secrets have been released to the general cave diving community. A recent check of the NACD website revealed more than twenty maps available for purchase. In the past, these maps were infrequently distributed, but now, many weekend enthusiasts use them as virtual check-off lists. Instead of learning the cave slowly by discovery, impatient divers choose to tick-off different tunnels from their map as they "conquer and move on." Maps can be extremely useful tools when used judiciously, but when divers exceed their training and experience, there can be deadly consequences.

Almost thirty years ago, training for cave divers was limited to an apprenticeship with experienced cave divers. Like surfers who defend their right to certain waves, cave divers policed their own ranks and kept divers in their place. Instructors from the NSS-CDS were not permitted to advertise or recruit students, but only reluctantly teach those that might come to harm if not corrected. In the last decade or so many corporations have jumped into the training game, adding hundreds of cave diving instructors to their ranks. Today's neophyte must carefully interview and select an instructor who not only has teaching credentials, but also a wide range of diving experiences in the overhead environment.

It is doubtful that cave diving records can sustain an exponential increase much longer. Yet, with the help of rebreathers and spirited teamwork, Jarrod

Jablonski, Casey McKinlay and a dedicated group from the Woodville Karst Plain Project have logged penetrations well over 20,000 feet. Young explorers in Mexico have linked neighboring systems, and mapped single caves to lengths well over 500,000 feet. Jason Mallinson with his support team has recorded unmatched distances in Pozo Azul in Spain. But it's not always the long distances that are the most remarkable. It's the fact that there are no limits to previously explored caves. Deep cavers like Richard Harris and Craig Challen, have not been afraid to push line 600 feet deep. Inventors, like Rick Stanton, have expanded the parameters of life support by using homemade micro-rebreathers. Sassy sidemounters, like Agnes Milowka, have never been bridled by limits to their imagination.

Within the bounds of a popular Florida state park's restricted zone, Milowka rumbles her old van through overgrown pastures and woodland and arrives at a stunning oasis. Patchy heirloom crops hint at the previous existence of the earliest settlers, the Timmucuan Indians. Remnants of later civilizations litter the spring basin; an old timber, leather boot soles and dull brass buttons from a soldier's uniform. Centuries ago, at this spring, a Spanish Mission was built, thrived and was subsequently destroyed by the native people it attempted to tame. It's a wild and beautiful place.

Agnes, a native Australian, begins her dive, stripped of all but a wetsuit, then digs her way into the crumbling passage. The tank she pushes ahead of her sustains her tiny 110-pound frame. She doesn't know that countless divers have already given up on this squeeze. She doesn't care that she's trespassing on state property. She doesn't even worry that if she has a bad day, her body won't be recovered. She just presses on, exploring in a vacuum, moving ahead because nobody has stopped her. She's made choices that few would make. The risks are her own and perhaps only engaged in the invincibility of youth. But despite taking risks some might call insane, she hits pay dirt and reveals another 8,500 feet of the mysterious conduits inside Mother Earth. Is it prudent? The community will undoubtedly judge her actions as either heroic or psychotic. Although reliable technology and tools have increased the range of modern cave divers, some things will never change. Wes Skiles' unlikely protégé will agree that, "Nothing can beat the moment you unwind a reel into completely uncharted territory."

This book reveals the fundamentals of cave training, while also delving into the edgier topics that pepper our sport today. If you are new to the sport, it will offer you the basics. If you have been cave diving for thirty years, it will welcome you into the fold of today's state-of-the-art explorers.

In July 2010 I received a phone call I never expected. My dear friend and creative partner Wes Skiles was dead. Though not cave diving, he was diving solo while filming with a rebreather on a shallow reef on the east coast of Florida. Then, just over six months after his death, I received a phone call that was not unexpected. My dear friend Agnes Milowka died conducting solo exploration activities in Tank Cave in Australia. She had entered a tiny passage, pushing a single tank ahead of her. She perished wedged in that passage, running out of air.

In my original foreword, I mentioned that the risks that Agnes took were her own, but I now have a much deeper understanding of our personal assessment of risk. Our decisions have wide implications that spill messily onto friends, family, cave rescue personnel and the entire community. Families and friends mourn. Divers quit doing what they love. Sites get closed. Recovery divers risk their lives. Innocent friends get swept into endless lawsuits. When somebody dies underwater, the scars are deep and permanent. I've lost at least three friends each year since the first release of this book. I hope that you consider them, your community and your loved ones every time you dive. Cave diving can be incredibly fulfilling, but prudence is best kept in the front of your mind.

Wes Skiles films the author and Dr. Tom Iliffe while working on a cave diving expedition and documentary film project in Bermuda. Photo: Nate Skiles

WHAT IS
CAVE DIVING?

CHAPTER 2

What is Cave Diving?------------------------------

Cave diving is a type of technical diving in which specialized equipment is used, enabling the exploration of natural overhead environments, which are at least partially filled with water. Some cave divers claim their roots in the sport of dry caving, but more often, they come from the ranks of sport divers, looking to extend their experience into new, more challenging environments.

To divers, caves are overhead environments that are void of light. Caverns occupy the daylight zone of caves, and as a result, cavern diving is only conducted during the daytime.

Caves have always engendered fascination, as sources of water flow, cultural vessels and geologic mysteries. Their extensive exploration is recent and like the great oceans, caves are one of the last frontiers for discovery on earth.

It has been said that we know more about outer space than inner earth, yet the science of "what happens underground" becomes more relevant as we try to protect vital resources such as drinking water. Formerly seen as adrenaline junkies, cave divers have become important, skilled volunteers for scientific investigations. Many cave divers are also reasonable voices in the area of water conservation and resource protection.

Divers take up the sport for a variety of reasons. It is regarded as the pinnacle of technical diving and tests the skills and awareness of even the best divers. Some divers are attracted to caves as dependable environments that tend to be open year-round, far from the effects of ocean waves. In many cases, divers drive to the edge of the water and jump into the most spectacular diving environments on earth. As great sources of mystery, they are alluring, challenging and dangerous. Underwater caves are a passion for some and obsession for others who explore their dark recesses.

La Sirena Cave in the Dominican Republic. Photo: Jill Heinerth

History of the Sport

Any attempt to fully describe the history of our sport will result in errors of omission and dating of this publication. Cave diving is evolving rapidly and records are shattered, almost daily. Exploration continues around the planet and technology is becoming ever-present in all aspects of cave diving. Training programs expand and reach wider audiences with general classes as well as specialty activities. Even with the population of active recreational divers in decline, technical and cave diving is experiencing growth.

The genesis of organized cave diving can be found in the United Kingdom, where divers formed the Cave Diving Group (CDG) in 1935. In 1936, Jack Sheppard used a homemade drysuit fed by a modified surface pump to walk through a sump, in the Mendip Hills. By the 1940s, this same group was exploring Wookey Hole and other sumps using military surplus rebreathers.

Dr. Bill Stone and his team from Stone Aerospace deploy the first artificially intelligent 3D robotic cave mapper in the fall of 2016 at Peacock Springs, Florida. Photo: Jill Heinerth

Cave diving became popularized in the early 1970s in the United States and began to gain a foothold in other countries such as Australia, France and the Bahamas. During this period of development many divers died due to lack of training and primitive equipment. Cave divers got organized, formed groups and developed training standards that made the sport safer in the 1980s. Led by American pioneering diver Sheck Exley, accident analysis became the foundation upon which most training was built.

In recent decades, cave diving has spread around the world. Most notably, the Mexican cenotes attract explorers to the Yucatan peninsula, creating an expansive tourism industry in region of the Riviera Maya. Nations from Poland to China and Norway to France have built cave diving groups and training organizations.

A significant project to archive the events of cave diving history has been created on the Internet at www.CaveDivingHistory.com, but legendary Welsh explorer, Martyn Farr is best known as the historian of cave diving. His book, "The Darkness Beckons," represents the best resource, documenting the history of our sport. A new edition of his book will be available late in 2017.

Engineer and designer Corey Jaskolski uses a Microsoft Hololens to view artifacts he has just scanned inside the cave entrance that lies behind archaeologist and National Geographic Explorer Guillermo de Anda (seated). Users of the Hololens can view these interactive high-resolution scans as augmented reality assets projected within the real environment. Check out the future of AR and cave exploration at www.DigitalPreservation.org.

THE TRAINING PROGRESSION

CHAPTER 3

The Training Progression------------------------

Cave diver training is comprised of several levels. Depending on the training agency, prerequisites may vary, contingent on whether you are taking training in stages or are progressing all the way through one integrated program.

Even before your first class, there are important physical skills and basic technical knowledge that should be mastered. Prior to training in any overhead environment your buoyancy control must be second nature. You must be comfortably weighted and trimmed even when your tanks are near empty. Equipment handling and self-sufficiency must be evident and your diving experience should satisfy your instructor that you are confident enough to manage emergencies in an environment that prohibits immediate access to the surface. Various agencies require a range from 10 to 100 dives as prerequisite for entry-level training and it is prudent to base your readiness on your experience, skills and comfort.

Cavern Diver

The first level of training is the Cavern Diver class. This program exposes divers to the overhead environment in very limited penetrations. It is intended to introduce basic skills and knowledge while building a foundation for cave diving. As with most cave diving programs, the lectures are built on a base of accident analysis. Careful review of accidents and incidents assists the student diver in learning about risk assessment and management while building awareness of safety procedures. Special focus is spent on buoyancy, trim, task loading, propulsion techniques and emergency skills. Dive planning, procedures, techniques, problem solving and conservation are covered in lecture sessions and practical training.

Taking approximately two days to complete, the class usually begins with lectures and dry-land scenarios, where students practice guideline procedures and emergency drills prior to entering the water.

The following limitations are imposed to keep cavern divers within a safe distance from the entrance:

- All diving is done within the range of the daylight zone of the cavern, so that at any point during their dive, a cavern diver may use daylight to reach the exit.

- All dives are confined to a maximum depth of 100 feet/30 meters and are limited to a total penetration of, distance plus depth, not to exceed 200 feet/65 meters.

- No decompression is permitted.

- No restrictions that require a team to swim single file are permitted.

- Penetration distances are limited to one third of a single tank or one sixth of a set of doubles or roughly 30 cubic feet of breathing gas.

- No complex navigation such as traverses, circuits or exploration.

Equipment for Cavern Diving

A recreational cavern class may be completed using a single scuba cylinder, but many divers opt for technical double tank configurations. Some training organizations do not allow CCR use, while others will permit training, but not offer certification until fully completing CCR cave diver training.

Students should be equipped with the following items:

- Mask and fins. Spring straps or taped straps are preferred for fins and durable neoprene mask straps are suggested over standard silicone or rubber straps.

- Tank configurations should carry a minimum of 72 cft/2000 L with a minimum starting pressure of 2000 psi/140 bar.

- Buoyancy device such as wings or BCD with adequate lift for the chosen tank(s).

- Tank plate and harness or BCD or integrated pack, suitable for attachment to the chosen tank(s).

Renee Power prepares for a cavern dive at Ginnie Springs, Florida. Photo: Jill Heinerth

- First stage regulators should be high performance types with a total of 2 second stages, with one of those being attached to a long hose of a minimum length of 5 feet/1.5 meters and a preferred length of 7 feet/2 meters. The regulator should be equipped with a submersible pressure gauge, a power inflation hose and optional drysuit inflation hose if applicable.

- Two battery-operated diving lights with a burn time that is suitable to exceed the planned dive time. Pistol and lantern grip lights are not recommended because of the challenge of using these lights while running a reel and because they are bulky when clipped to the diver.

- Safety reel/spool with at least 100 feet/30 meters of double-braided line.

- Dive computer or timing device with depth gauge.

- Submersible dive tables or electronic dive planner or backup computer.

- Slate or notebook, pencil.

A wrist slate offers you the chance to take notes without having to dig into a pocket each time. Photo: Jill Heinerth

- A small knife or cutting tool, designed to minimize entanglement and maximize access (two cutting tools preferred).

- Wet or drysuit appropriate for the planned dive durations. A hood is recommended for thermal and impact protection.

- One primary diving reel with a minimum length of 350 feet/110 meters of double-braided line per team.

- Appropriate weight belt or harness if needed.

Most training agencies require the student to be at least 18 years of age, although some allow special waivers for younger participants. In these cases, parents must be carefully briefed on risks so that they are fully aware of the dangers their child may be facing. Although young people tend to have excellent manual diving skills, they may lack the maturity necessary to fully understand and accept the risks associated with overhead environment diving.

At all times during a cavern dive, the team should be able to see, both the daylight, and the guideline leading to the exit. Photo: Jill Heinerth

Introduction to Cave Diving/Basic Cave Diver/Cave One

The second step of training for most agencies is called Introduction to Cave Diving/Basic Cave Diver or Cave One. In some cases this level of training may be completed using a single tank with dual outlet valve, such as a Y- or H-valve but most people use double tank configurations. Some agencies permit experienced rebreather divers to use an approved rebreather system with bailout gas. Each training agency has different limitations at this level. Generally, the single tank cave diver can earn a permanent certification. Divers that opt for double tank training may earn a card with a one-year to 18-month expiration in some cases. CCR divers are usually not offered a certification card at this level but are registered as being at a transitional point of their training. In all cases, divers are encouraged to continue their education. Most professionals feel that, although students are offered the fundamentals of cave diving, they are at an increased risk in the overhead environment if they do not further their training as cave divers. Completion of the entire set of programs is highly endorsed.

At this level of training, many of the essential skills taught at the cavern level are refined and improved. Elementary cave dives are completed while staying within the limits of the main line and linear penetration. More time is spent on topics including geology, hydrology, conservation, procedures, techniques, problem solving and crisis management. Special emphasis is focused on swim technique, buoyancy and trim while stressing the reduction of silting, especially under task loads and in emergency scenarios.

Ordinarily taking at least two days to complete after a cavern level class, the program is conducted at sites beyond the scope of caverns. Instructors ensure there that their students gain experience in new, more advanced environments with new challenges such as silt, low flow, high flow, tides or formations. Advanced scuba training and Nitrox qualification is recommended, if not required, by training agencies.

The following limitations are imposed to establish the safe range for training and experience for Intro/Basic Cave Divers.

- Dives are limited to a maximum depth of 100 feet/30 meters.

- 30 feet/9 meters of starting visibility.

- No decompression is allowed.

- No restrictions that would force a dive team to swim in single file.

- Penetration distances are limited to one third of a single tank, or one sixth of a set of doubles, or roughly 30 cubic feet of gas.

- Single tanks should have a minimum of 70 cft/2000 L with a minimum starting pressure of 2000 psi/140 bar. Doubles should have a minimum starting pressure of 1800 psi/120 bar although single tank programs at this level are becoming increasingly rare.

- No complex navigation such as traverses, circuits or exploration are allowed. No jumps or gaps are permitted and all penetration should occur on the main guideline. (Note: A jump reel is used to conduct lost diver drills, but this reel is never tied into a secondary passage for further penetration.

- No diver propulsion vehicles or other task-loading devices are permitted.

Equipment for Intro/Basic Cave Diving

The Intro/Basic Cave Diving student will be equipped with the following items:

- Mask and fins. Spring straps or taped straps are preferred for fins and durable neoprene mask straps are preferred over silicone or rubber.

- Tank configurations should carry a minimum of 70 cft/2000 L with a minimum starting pressure of 2000 psi/140 bar. If the student chooses a single tank configuration, it must be equipped with a dual-outlet valve.

- Buoyancy device such as wings or BCD, adequate for flotation of the chosen tank(s), with backmounted wings being preferred. Some agencies require dual, redundant wings for students wearing wetsuits.

- Tank plate and harness or BCD or integrated pack suitable for attachment to the chosen tank(s).

- Two, first-stage, high performance regulators with a total of two, second-stages, with one of those being attached to a long hose of a minimum length of 7 feet/2 meters. The regulators should be equipped with one submersible pressure gauge, one power inflation hose with a drysuit inflation hose if applicable. DIN-type connections are highly recommended over yoke attachments.

- One primary diving light, adequate for the intended dive duration. Pistol and lantern grip lights are not recommended because of the challenge of using these lights with a reel and the bulky storage when clipped to the diver.

- Two battery-operated backup diving lights with a burn time that exceeds the planned dive time(s).

- Safety reel or spool with at least 100 feet/30 meters of double-braided guideline.

- Dive computer or timing device with depth gauge, slate, pencil and submersible dive tables. Consoles gauges are generally discouraged.

- Backup computer or bottom timer with depth gauge and backup tables.

- One or two small harness-mounted knives or cutting tools designed to minimize entanglement.

 - Wet or drysuit appropriate for the planned dive durations with a hood for impact protection and warmth.

 - One primary diving reel with a minimum length of 350 feet/110 meters of double-braided line per team.

 - Optional backup mask.

 - At least three directional line arrows and three non-directional markers such as cookies or clothes pins, depending on regional preference.

Many instructors choose to combine the Cavern and Intro/Basic level into a three to five day course. Divers who plan to continue to the next level of training immediately, often take a break after this class for further practice/recovery.

Cave One

Some agencies, such as NAUI, RAID and GUE, subdivide their training a little differently. Similar to Basic or Intro to Cave, this level may be conducted in a single or double tank, open circuit configuration, and requires a dual outlet valve in either case. Most dive sites treat this as an equivalent to Basic or Intro, even though it tends to take a little more training time and includes a few ad-

ditional skills. All diving is restricted to linear penetration on the main line. Gear requirements are similar to those listed above.

It is prudent to gain experience before moving on to the next level. Remain within the limits of linear penetration of the cave and stay conservative. Photo: Jill Heinerth

31

Apprentice Cave Diver

The Apprentice Cave Diver level is the third in the series of training programs. This class introduces advanced navigation, longer penetrations and more refined skills. The program focuses on dive planning and preparation for longer dives including decompression. Emphasis is placed on achieving excellence in general skills with exposure to new caves and more advanced environments. A time limited training recognition may be issued on successful completion of the program, but divers are encouraged to move on to complete Full Cave Diver training in fairly short order. Ordinarily, this stage of training is considered to expire in one year, or eighteen months if a diver chooses to take a break. The equipment requirements are the same as previous levels with the addition of a decompression/safety bottle and recommended oxygen analyzer, additional gap reels and spools that enable the diver to begin making jumps off of the main guideline. Penetrations are extended to a maximum of one third of a set of double tanks.

Cave Diver/Full Cave/Cave Two

The Cave Diver level is also known as Full Cave or Cave Two. This level is recognized as the completion of cave training. With this qualification card, divers may gain unrestricted access to most cave diving sites. During this phase of training, students experience complex dive plans including circuits, traverses, decompression and demanding environmental conditions. Jump reels and decompression tanks are added to the equipment list. RAID adds skills involving stage bottles as well. Emphasis is placed on experiencing a wide variety of circumstances that will prepare the individual to dive in a wide range of locations.

After completion of training, it is suggested that divers remain with limits that include:

- Penetrations of a maximum of one third of a set of double tanks.

- Depths not exceeding 130 feet/40 meters.

- 20 feet/6 meters of starting visibility.

- No complex tasks such as DPV use, gear removal or exploration.

- For RAID Cave Two divers, use of a stage bottle is permitted if it has the same gas as the primary tanks.

Training Organizations Around the World

The National Speleological Society - Cave Diving Section (NSS-CDS)

Founded in 1941, The National Speleological Society (NSS) unites thousands of individuals dedicated to the safe study, exploration, and conservation of caves. The NSS promotes a variety of scientific, educational, and conservation projects - including grants and scholarships to professional and student biolo-gists, geologists, hydrologists, and archaeologists for cave-related research; purchase of cave properties for the public trust; conservation studies, cleanups, and restorations; a nationwide rescue-and-recovery network; and a multitude of publications concerning all aspects of cave science, exploration, survey, cartography, photography, and physical techniques.

By 1973, in response to meeting the specific needs of cave divers, the NSS formed the Cave Diving Section (NSS-CDS). The NSS-CDS is the largest cave diving organization in the U.S. with members in almost every state and around the world. In 1983 the Cave Diving Section was independently incorporated and in 1987 was granted official nonprofit, tax-exempt status as a scientific and educational organization. Beyond training, the CDS has a special interest in maintaining and acquiring cave diving sites and in conservation. **www.nsscds.org**

National Association for Cave Diving (NACD)

During August 1968, several experienced cave divers held a meeting at Hornsby Spring near the town of High Springs, Florida. They addressed the growing number of fatalities in caves. With the in-volvement of law enforcement, government and open water interests, it became clear that the best solution would be the development of nationally recognized training standards for cave diving. On May 15, 1969, the National Association for Cave Diving (NACD) was officially incorporated. As a pioneer in cave training, education, exploration and  research, the NACD aims to promote safety, encourage training and dissemination of information as well supports cooperation with other diving communities, the government and private interests. **www.safecavediving.com**

Cave Divers Association of Australia (CDAA)

The CDAA was formed in September 1973. Similar to the situation in North America, landowners throughout the Mount Gambier region of South Australia were considering the closure of dive sites following a number of diving fatalities. The newly formed organization defined a series of criteria and testing procedures. Initially this was a listing of all the popular cave diving sites divided into three different categories based on their degree of difficulty. Cards were issued to divers to indicate their competency to landowners. The landowners gradually gained confidence in the ability of the CDAA to train safe cave divers and, as a result, the sites remained open.

The main aims and objectives of the CDAA today are to foster the development, advancement, promotion, mapping, education, exploration, conservation, safety and research of underwater caves and related features.

www.cavedivers.com/au

Australians divide training into several levels that include: Deep Cavern, Cave and Advanced Cave Diver. All sites are rated according to their level of technical difficulty. To dive at a site in a particular range of difficulty, the diver must provide proof of training completion and, in some cases, experience in other locations of a similar level. The four categories are Cavern, Sinkhole, Cave and Advanced Cave (previously Penetration).

Australian cave diving instructors John Vanderleest and Linda Claridge swim through Tank Cave in Australia's Mount Gambier region. The extensive system offers plenty of opportunities for complex navigation. Visitors to Australia need to apply for a special permit to dive in caves that are governed by the CDAA and most cave dives are conducted on a guided basis. Photo: Jill Heinerth

Cave Diving Group (CDG)

The Cave Diving Group (CDG) is a United Kingdom-based diver training organization specializing in cave diving. The organization was founded in 1946 by Graham Balcombe, making it the world's oldest cave diving club. Graham

Balcombe and Jack Sheppard pioneered cave diving in the late 1930s, notably at Wookey Hole Caves in Somerset. The organization focuses as much on dry-caving and sump techniques as crisis management training and cave diver education. **http://cavedivinggroup.org.uk**

The CDG works on a mentoring and apprenticeship format. All cave divers in this organization first prove their competence as dry cavers, since many of the British caves involve sump exploration in challenging conditions. Diving is almost secondary to perfection of critical caving skills and exploration and risk management. The group offers several classes of membership to include divers, temporary permit holders and non-divers but discourages recreational cave divers from participation in diving activities in UK caves.

RAID

RAID is a quickly growing international training agency offering courses broken into the tiered Cave One/Cave Two system. They offer a decidedly international approach to offering the most conservative practices in cave diving that reflect different conditions and procedures used around the world. They are unique in their approach to online training and record keeping. **www.DiveRaid.com**

Agencies and Regional Organizations

Most corporate scuba training agencies offer cave diver training, including, but not limited to: IANTD, NAUI, PADI, PSAI, CMAS, GUE and TDI/SDI. Other smaller, geographically specific nonprofit cave diving organizations exist with a special focus on regional characteristics of caves. In Scandinavia and some parts of Europe, natural caves are rare. Specialized training has been developed for complex, flooded mines in the region. In Mexico, special emphasis is placed on protecting delicate speleothems, while training in locations with offshore ocean caves may require a solid understanding of the influence of tides on caves.

Mexico's Riviera Maya is a very popular region for cave diving and training. Photo of pioneering cave explorer Kay Walten by Jill Heinerth

Preparation

Before any class you should:

- Read the text(s) that are recommended by your instructor.

- Complete any online homework, quizzes or tests that are required by your agency.

- Prepare and inspect your equipment to ensure it is properly maintained.

- Practice your buoyancy techniques in the gear you wish to use.

- Review academic topics like Nitrox and decompression, if applicable for your level of training.

- Get a medical check to ensure fitness for cave diving and have your doctor sign an appropriate RSTC medical approval form or similar document.

- Be fit, rested and properly hydrated.

Choosing an Instructor

Your choice for a cave diving instructor is very important. First, they should be a good fit with your diving philosophy. They should dive in caves regularly, outside of teaching activities. Your instructor must be insured and should charge a professional rate that supports their dedication to the craft. It is your right to interview your instructor about their diving background and experiences outside of teaching. You are making an investment in life support education.

Determine what type of equipment your instructor is using actively in the cave. Are they diving backmount, sidemount or rebreather? Especially at the early levels of training, it is very valuable to take a class from someone who is using similar equipment to yours. Watching a role model swim through the cave can be extremely valuable. Photo of Jakub Rehacek from Golem Gear using a Flex sidemount rebreather by Jill Heinerth.

Beyond the Essentials

After gaining experience as a cave diver, many people choose to embark on new adventures and continuing education. Specialty programs have been devised for numerous areas of interest including: survey, stage diving, cartography, sidemount technique, photography, trimix, DPV, rebreathers and other activities. These are discussed in detail in Chapter Ten.

Cave Diving Guides

When traveling around the world to new caves, divers should seek local knowledge. Protocols differ as much as the caves themselves. Divers in sea caves may find heavy polypropylene line in use to protect against marine growth. Line arrows simply won't fit on this type of line. Tides may present further difficulties. Australians use clothespins to mark jumps and Ts, which are numerous at their most popular site Tank Cave. Cold weather destinations tend to permanently "T" the line instead of creating jumps and gaps. I have seen wire guideline in Russia, ski rope in Canada and sponge-encrusted line in Bermuda. The traveling cave diver should be prepared to seek guidance from locals or be prepared to modify their technique to suit local conditions.

Local guides may help you gain access to unique sites, brief you on entry considerations and even act as a trained dive buddy. It is important to review their credentials and background (as you would for any dive buddy) to ensure they are properly trained and share the same regard for safety that you do. Even if you dive with a guide, you must conduct your dives with the assumption that you need to be capable of self-rescue and buddy-rescue, if the need arises. Don't let the relaxation of vacation diving lure you in to complacency. A guide in a foreign country will want to take you on the most thrilling dive of your life. It is your responsibility to make sure it is not your last.

After numerous fatalities and incidents in the Yucatan, Mexican dive operators formed an organization called APSA (Asociacion de Prestadores de Servicios Acuaticos). These business professionals set quality control standards for service and safety, establishing strict requirements for guiding and teaching in caverns and caves. Not many countries offer this level of organization for cave

guides though, so you will need to be very diligent when hiring a personal guide.

Recently, the NSS-CDS developed a mentoring program to train card-carrying Cave Diving Supervisors. This program is designed to provide training in dive leadership to competent, certified cave divers who will lead or guide other certified cave divers on cave dives. A Cave Diver Supervisor is a leadership or instructor-in-training rating.

The program is designed to assist in the development of a formal guide training program for the various properties with cave diving sites owned and/or managed by the NSS-CDS, so as to ensure consistency in regard to cave diving skills, safety and techniques.

Your cave diving guide is your partner. You should never relinquish your responsibility of navigation to participate in a "Trust-Me-Dive." Don't allow the vacation state of mind to place you in danger. Your guide is not infallible. Photo of cave instructors Pam Wooten and Garry Dallas by Jill Heinerth.

ACCIDENT
ANALYSIS

CHAPTER

4

Learning from Accident Analysis-------------

In 1973, the number of fatalities that were occurring in caves alarmed a pioneering cave diver named Sheck Exley. A high school math teacher by trade, Exley had a fascination, and some would say obsession with statistics. He carefully tracked records, logs and the minutia of exploration throughout his career. Exley's greatest gift to the dive community was his thoughtful review of accidents and incidents, which he organized into a series of root causes. In his first assessment, he determined the most likely causes of death for divers with no experience or training in caves. He summarized these as follows:

Training

The greatest common denominator between accidents was the lack of training in techniques suitable for the overhead environment. In fact, many of the deceased were highly experienced open water divers, even instructors, who simply had no experience in caves. Caves were rumored to be dark, frightening places where silt would engulf a diver in an inescapable claustrophobic nightmare. Experienced divers visiting the pure and alluring Florida springs did not perceive these stunning places as dangerous. They were tempted by the false comfort of crystal, clear spring water welling up in the entrances. But without training, it was easy to become lost or disoriented in the maze of passages, kick up silt, or simply fail to reserve enough gas to get out.

Guideline

Failure to run a continuous guideline to the open water was the second most common factor in accidents and the greatest *direct* cause of fatalities. The lure of clear water drew divers further into the cave than they could safely return by memory. Without a reference back to open water the divers became lost.

Running a reel from the open water to the permanent guideline ensures the ability to exit using the line as a tactile reference. Numerous complacent divers failed to run these guidelines and reels to cover jumps in the cave and subsequently died. Visual jumps have Photo: Jill Heinerth

Gas

The third most common cause of death was a failure to reserve enough gas for exit. Equipment was less reliable in the early days of cave diving and gear failures were common. Open water divers, accustomed to the habit of turning around with slightly more than half their pressure did not retain enough gas volume to deal with a buddy emergency or increased respiration due to stress. Many early fatalities occurred close to the entrance since divers were scrambling to get out, sharing air and stretching dwindling supplies beyond their limits.

Depth

Many fatalities occurred at depths exceeding 150 feet/45 meters. Air dives with air decompression were the norm. Narcosis contributed to some of these fatalities and lack of time to deal with crises made deep diving a high-risk activity.

Lights

The final issue cited by Exley, was the failure to carry at least three lights. Quality cave diving lights were hard to find, negatively buoyant and expensive. Recreational divers were not likely to own proper lighting, and in several cases, a team of divers shared one or two lights. Equipment failures likely left these divers lost in the darkness of the cave.

Fatalities of Trained Cave Divers

Accident Analysis

A new training regimen emerged that was based on correcting the faults identified in Exley's accident analysis. Experienced divers were still dying in unacceptable numbers, so Exley further examined their deaths in order to form a new list of root causes.

For trained cave divers, exceeding experience and training levels, along with complacency, appears to be much more of an issue. Roughly 80 percent of fatalities occur at depths greater than 150 feet/45 meters. In our early history, many deaths were associated with narcosis and deep air diving. These days, some are attributed to improper gas choice, but the time pressure of dealing with emergencies in deep water is also a factor. There is very little time available to make good decisions and retreat from gas supply emergencies. Extensive training, experience and practice are needed for cave dives below 130 feet/40 meters.

The second leading cause of fatalities of trained cave divers is associated with guideline issues and the failure to run a continuous guideline to open water. These preventable situations arise from complacency. Some divers fail to properly mark Ts, jumps and gaps. Other accidents occurred when divers conducted "visual gaps," reasoning that familiarity with an area negated the need for standard safety protocols. Others simply skipped running a reel to connect the main line with the open water or safe ascent zone. There is no excuse for laziness when running a reel could save the life of a diver trying to exit in decreased visibility. When an emergency causes perceptual narrowing, a reel can make the difference between confusion and survival.

The third killer of trained cave divers is failure to reserve adequate gas for exit from the cave. It is easy to understand the psychology of such an error. A particular team member, who uses more gas than the others, may always be in the position to call the dive. If he is teased, he may get weary of being the person who always limits the group from penetrating further into the cave. At some point, a barrier is reached and until extra equipment and gas is employed, it will not be breached. The temptation to push a little further can be irresistible. But cutting it close by "pushing thirds" is not a risk taken by an individual for their own sake. When thirds are exceeded, it is the entire team that is left short.

Some rebreather cave divers have perished when they failed to carry enough open circuit bailout gas to ensure a safe exit in the event of a complete rebreather failure. Photo of rebreather bailout tanks stages at Stargate Cave in Andros, Bahamas by Jill Heinerth.

Activities such as aviation and surgery have significantly improved their safety record by insisting on the use of checklists. Photo: Jill Heinerth

A growing number of cave divers are dying while diving solo. Solo diving is not the *direct* cause of their demise, but rather, a contributory factor, since equipment and gas supply redundancy is minimized. Many cave divers practice the sport without a dive buddy, but the prudent ones do so with extra conservatism and additional gas supplies and gear. At least two prominent cave divers (one a cave diving instructor) have perished while solo diving and using a "half, plus 200 psi" turn philosophy, reasoning that there is nobody who will need the reserve gas. The solo diver, left without a redundant brain, is more prone to make an unrecoverable mistake and often pushes the limits or general rules of cave diving. When a solo diver dies just three feet short of his next stage bottle, it is not the solo effort that killed him, but rather, an inadequate air supply for the dive as planned. Successful solo dives must be carefully planned with additional risks assumed by the diver. Some instructors and agencies have added "solo diving" to their list of killers, but it remains an *indirect* contributor to fatalities.

Driving a DPV is an advanced activity that requires additional training, experience and enhanced dive planning. Although DPVs are generally reliable, they may leave you stranded a long way from an exit. Gas planning is critical for all possible abort scenarios. Photo: Patty Mortara

Modern Factors

These days, recovery divers are more likely to retrieve a body from deep within a cave system where a technical diver may have used a rebreather, scooter or other advanced exploration technique to gain penetration distance. Accidents involving recreational divers have decreased significantly, but trained cave divers, extending beyond their experience and training seem more likely to meet their demise. Like everything else about our modern world, humans seem inclined to push the limits and are impatient about training for new experiences. Rather than progressively learning a cave system step by

step, divers seem more apt to use maps to check off a long list of destinations. Cave diving for some, is more about the ultimate destination rather than the journey. This philosophy is getting divers into trouble. On one hand, I salute people who push the limits of humankind's imagination, however, cautious divers will do well to slow down and enjoy the learning curve before engaging in deep penetration and/or exploration dives.

Long-range DPVs ferry divers to extreme distances, presenting significant risk to a recovery team in the event of an accident. Photo of Jill Heinerth entering the cave on an exploration dive of Wakulla Springs by Richard Nordstrom.

GEOLOGY &
HYDROLOGY

CHAPTER 5

Geology and Hydrology------------------------------

A rudimentary understanding of geology and cave formation provides a cave diver with an enhanced awareness of their environment. Basic knowledge assists the diver in making good risk assessment choices, aids in navigation and adds to the enjoyment of diving. With an apology to scientists everywhere, I present this chapter as general knowledge, with the understanding that cave divers have created their own vernacular that may differ from scientific terminology. Geology is a highly specialized discipline and well beyond the scope of most cave diving classes.

It is prudent for divers to reconsider the meaning of the term "geologic time." Scientists often use these words to describe activities that occurred over a long period of time or things that happened a long time ago. For cave divers, we must remember that "geologic time" includes right now. The cave you dived in a few weeks ago may not be the same on your next visit. There are many factors that can affect the morphology or stability of a cave including floods, drought, seismic activities or local occurrences. Dives with complex navigation should be carefully set up with safety and conservatism in mind. Never enter a cave at one entrance on the assumption that you will be able to exit at another location without preparing for success first. This topic will be covered further in the section on complex navigation that includes diagrams for circuits and traverses.

Cave Diving Regions of the World

Submerged caves are found throughout the world, but infrastructure and access are often the limiting factors for cave divers. As passion for the sport expands, new regions of exploration are constantly opening. At the time of this writing some of the most active regions for cave divers include: Florida, Missouri, Mexico, Bahamas, Belize, Brazil, Bermuda, France, UK, Spain, Italy, Czech Republic, Australia, Hungary and Russia with burgeoning areas in China, Thailand, Cuba, Papua New Guinea, Scandinavia, and the Ukraine. Most caves are found in areas rich in limestone, but other types of caves are worthy of exploration.

Mines

Cave divers are also diving in abandoned, flooded mines around the world. They contain many of the same hazards as natural caves swell as hazards created by manmade objects within their depths. Cave diving techniques translate well to these locations with an added caution to consider entanglement from remaining equipment and abandoned electrical supplies. Mines may also have stability issues. It is generally advisable to stay away from contact with walls since rock falls can occur. Local guides can offer assistance in these unique environments.

Types of Underwater Caves

Coral Caves

Many divers have their first experience in the overhead environment in coral caves. These formations are typically found beneath living coral structures, when arching branches of Elkhorn coral or large sheets of plate corals enclose a corridor of sea floor. Some offshore reefs are referred to as spur and groove

formations. Running per-pendicular to shore, these ridges of coral are interspersed with sand hallways. As the reef matures, the reefs grow into a canopy, much like arching trees over a country road. Daylight often dapples through small openings and lengthy passages are rare.

A coral cavern in the Florida Keys is filled with silverside baitfish. Photo: Jill Heinerth

Although getting lost is not likely, there are other specific hazards to this environment. With passages often running perpendicular to shore, they can be subject to dramatic surge, which can push the diver against delicate corals and hydroids, damaging them and injuring the diver. Marine life may seek

refuge in these caverns so care should be taken when entering. Many years ago, I came face to face with a startled bull shark when I turned the corner in a coral cavern at a site called Snapper Hole on the east side of Grand Cayman. I'm not sure which of us was more surprised, but the large shark was somehow able to turn on a dime and disappear before I had time to think. My only thought at that tense moment was that I was extremely relieved that it wasn't a dead end tunnel!

Reneé Power enters a coral cave in Grand Cayman. Photo: Jill Heinerth

Sea Caves

The term sea cave is a bit of a misnomer since sea caves do not necessarily occur in the ocean. Sea caves are formed when wave action cuts a notch into a rocky escarpment at water level. Sea caves may become later submerged during different water stands and as a result, it is possible to find remnant sea caves at great depths on walls, such as the "Tongue of the Ocean" in the Bahamas. Sea caves may also be found in lakes. The North American Great Lakes are very large and therefore have very aggressive wave action that cuts into locations such as the Niagara Escarpment near Tobermory, Ontario, Canada. Sea caves may also be formed in a very short period of time in icebergs.

The genesis of a sea cave begins when wave action scores a notch in the landscape at sea level. Photo of Christmas Island sea cave by Jill Heinerth.

When entering active sea caves, divers should be wary of surge as well as tides. Anchoring a boat inside a sea cave may be risky. While exploring in Antarctica, my team entered an iceberg sea cave on a reasonably calm day to sample water chemistry. While motoring slowly into the entrance, a large rogue wave surged through the doorway almost pinning the crew and their Zodiac to the ceiling. Underwater, I felt considerably safer than the boaters!

Lava Tubes

Caves may be formed by volcanic activities. The most common type of volcanic cave is called a lava tube. When lava spills down the flank of an active volcano, the exterior of the flow cools before the interior of the tube. Hot lava rushes through the conduit; sometimes leaving a void after the eruption has subsided. When lava reaches the ocean, it hits the water causing a massive gas explosion, often vaporizing parts of the sea in its wake. If the flow continues below the surface of the water, the skin cools first and tunnels are left where the lava has continued moving down the slope. The longest known, submerged lava tube cave in the world is called Atlantida Tunnel, on the island of Lanzarote, off the western coast of Africa. The lava tube is over 7 km long with collapsed ceiling portals peppering the mountain and a lengthy portion running below the sea floor.

49

Dr. Tom Iliffe swims through Atlantida Cave on Lanzarote in the Canary Islands. Atlantida, Jameos del Agua or the Tunnel to Atlantis as it is known locally, is the longest submerged lava tuba cave in the world. Photo: Jill Heinerth

Fracture Caves

Some caves are found in fault lines and deep fractures. Andros Island and Iceland are common destinations for this type of diving. In Andros, fractures or slump faults run parallel to the shoreline and are generally only several hundred meters inland. They often intersect with other types of caves.

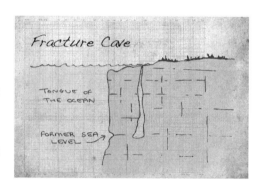

Iceland's Silfra Fracture is a remarkable environment, spreading slightly wider each year as the continental plates continue to separate. Photo: Jill Heinerth

In Silfra Fracture at Iceland's Thingvellir Lake National Park, you can dive in the rift between the North America and Eurasia continental plates. At this World Heritage Site, the plates move apart a little bit each day. As you swim through the crack you can place an outstretched arm on each continent. The majority of dives at this site occur within the view of daylight from above, but in places, a true cave scenario has developed when large boulders have fallen into fissures, creating elaborate swim throughs. As a geologically active area, Silfra is constantly evolving over time. Scientists are studying this unique site and the unusual flora and fauna that inhabit it.

Dissolution Caves

The longest and most complex type of caves occur where carbonate, sedimentary rocks, such as limestone or dolomite, have been dissolved by natural forces over time. These types of caves are found in landscape referred to as Karst terrain. The origin of the word

karst came from the Slavic region known as the Dinaric Kras. The word was later Germanized to karst and is now used to describe areas of carbonate platforms, which are subject to forces of dissolution.

Subterranean caverns, carved by groundwater, characterize karst topography. Many karst regions are dotted with sinkholes, cracks and fissures. Cave divers will often dive in springs and sinks in these regions.

Water has carved the passages in this region of the cave called The Catacombs in the Devil's System at Ginnie Springs, Florida. Photo: Jill Heinerth

Karst landscapes begin as submerged landmasses. Florida and the southeastern United States were once waterlogged, below the Tethys Sea. During this time, the calcified remains of sea creatures piled up on the sea floor and were compressed over time. During drier epochs, when sea levels retreated and exposed the Florida peninsula, the environment became subject to aggressive erosional forces. As rain fell on the sedimentary rock, it began to seep into the ground through a process known as percolation. As water travelled down through tiny spaces in between rocks and soil particles and within the sponge-like limestone rock, it carried with it carbon dioxide from the atmosphere and became slightly acidic. Additional carbon dioxide was picked up as well as sulfates, which increased the potency of the water's ability to dissolve limestone. Capitalizing on weak areas like cracks and fissures, water soaked into the ground and dissolved away the rock. In some levels, loosely packed layers, called bedding planes, were easily dissolved as the water attempted to follow the gradient of the land from higher elevations down towards its lowest point. Erosion continued over time above the water table as well as below, where complex underground drainage networks were formed. Drainage attempts to follow the path of least resistance, and where it runs into insoluble barriers, such as heavy clays, it may run over the top of those confining barriers or bypass around them to more soluble features. Speleogenesis is the geologic term that describes the formation of caves.

Sponge-like limestone is filled with many voids that easily store water. The water saturated rock makes up the vast Floridan Aquifer. Photo: Jill Heinerth

North Florida residents often inaccurately refer to spring and river levels as reliant on snow melt in faraway places. Yet, cave divers have assisted in unraveling the mysteries of regional and local watersheds through scientific examination and detailed survey work. We now understand that springs belong to a traceable region called a springshed. Groundwater can be dye-traced and a region of influence, known as a recharge area, can be defined for a spring.

Deep below the surface, water is trapped within permeable rock, such as limestone, or within the spaces between gravel, sand, silt or clay. These saturated zones, from which groundwater can be extracted through wells, is called an aquifer. The Floridan Aquifer is one of the world's most productive sources of water, extending below the state of Florida, and sections of Georgia,

Alabama and South Carolina. Groundwater within the Floridan Aquifer is held under pressure below a confining level of non-permeable sediments. When the water pressure is great enough, the groundwater gushes out of the ground as a spring. The volume of water flowing

Karst Window

from a spring is dependent upon a variety of factors: the water pressure in the aquifer, the number of conduits leading to a spring vent or opening, and the size of the opening itself. Florida's springs are the largest by volume in the world, giving birth to and supporting entire river ecosystems such as the Suwannee, Ichetucknee, Wakulla, Santa Fe and dozens more. Collectively, Florida's springs discharge over 19 billion gallons of freshwater each day through more than 600 notable openings.

Springs are classified based on the magnitude of their discharge. First magnitude springs such as Wakulla, Spring Creek, Weeki Wachee and Silver Springs, each express more than 65 million gallons of water per day (greater than 100 cu ft. per second). Volume of discharge varies over time and is dependent on rainfall, climate, aquifer pressure and withdrawals through water wells.

Over-permitting and withdrawals in addition to discharge of pollutants to the waterways and landscapes within the watershed threaten springs. Each day in Florida, as much as 8 billion gallons of water are removed from the aquifer for human consumption, agriculture and industry. Simultaneously, pollutants such as fertilizers, chemicals, pesticides, stormwater runoff and harmful materials are applied to the surface of the earth to be carried deep into the vaults of freshwater reserves that serve to refuel our springs. Cave divers have

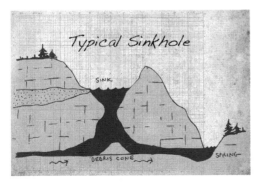

Typical Sinkhole

a unique responsibility to serve as ambassadors, sharing their knowledge and experience with the public. Cave divers have an opportunity to educate their communities, to protect fragile environments and safeguard the supply of freshwater for future generations.

Threats to Caves and Water Quality

Lawn Care and Landscaping

Certain methods of lawn care can have a detrimental effect on springs. Application of chemical pesticides and fertilizers often pass by the root zone and seep down into groundwater reserves. Components such as nitrates may be invisible, yet they feed nuisance algae that often choke the entrances of springs. Nitrates and toxins eventually flow downstream from the springs that serve as sources of major river ecosystems, feeding algae and exotic plants along the way. Eventually, overgrowth in the rivers can consume the oxygen within the water and result in collapse of the entire system.

Landscaping and lawn care also take a toll on the quantity of water available to the system. Floridians are some of the largest daily water consumers on the planet, with perhaps half of their withdrawals from the aquifer being used to maintain residential lawns, which in turn must be mowed, fertilized and treated with ever more dangerous pesticides.

Native, drought-tolerant species can be planted to create a beautiful residential landscape that is less of a strain on supplies and does not require application of fertilizers or insecticides. Slow-release and controlled-release fertilizers, used judiciously, may be a compromise solution for those that cannot part with their green-carpeted landscape.

Human Consumption

Besides nourishment, water is used in large quantities to fuel a modern household and groundwater is by far the least expensive source of water to satisfy the public's thirst. Conservation will soon be critical to retain the life we enjoy. Water managers carefully monitor flows and levels of some springs and rivers yet many conservationists know we have already permitted more withdrawal than is sustainable in aquifers all over the world. Some parts of the world have already suffered the impact of declining groundwater levels. Many Australians are forced to practice extremely stringent conservation. Bermudians rely solely on rainwater captured on rooftop collection systems. Many undeveloped regions of our planet survive on mere cups per day. Long-term conservation goals and practices will be essential to our survival.

Dumping

In the past, sinkholes have been used as refuse dumps. Landowners, unaware of their connection to water resources, saw these openings in the earth as convenient locations to discard their garbage. Whether a sinkhole contains water or not, its connection to the aquifer is now undisputed. Cleanup of these sites is underway in many communities, but identification, education and action are critically needed in all karst regions of the planet.

Agriculture

Like residential lawn care, farming has an impact on the quantity and quality of water flowing from the aquifer. That said, farmers are being more progressive about saving money and are therefore more likely to use fertilizers sparingly. Although a typical farm may apply one million gallons of water to crops daily, some of that soaks back into the ground. Additionally, many government programs help farmers to implement water-saving measures and other Best Management Practices that protect the quality of water resources. It can be argued that farming also sets aside large areas for healthy recharge of the aquifer and leaves a smaller carbon footprint on the planet by providing local food resources.

Livestock

Massive livestock operations need to dispose of large quantities of animal wastes. If these wastes are allowed to enter the aquifer through sinks or streams, or slowly descend through permeable soils, they can have an enormous impact on the quality of our water resources. Livestock also consume significant quantities of water. Responsible operators have found excellent solutions by containing wastes and manufacturing market-ready products from those wastes, thus removing the concentration from a particular watershed. Recycling of water in these operations is also a proven, positive conservation method. However, it is undisputed that a vegetarian lifestyle has a lower water and carbon footprint on the planet. Eating less meat in your diet actually conserves tremendous quantities of water.

Development and Stormwater

Population growth stresses both the quantity and quality of available water. As communities grow, recharge lands are often lost. Every tree pulls nitrogen out of the ground that might otherwise contaminate a spring. Every acre of open field that is paved over, adds to stormwater runoff. Thoughtful urban planning and reasonable water permit limits will be critical to springs protection. Deed-restricted communities will need to rethink their association's by-laws, which often promote pollution by requiring specific landscaping and lawn care techniques and standards.

When rainfall is not absorbed by soils and plants or gathered in natural water bodies and retention ponds, it often lands on paved surfaces such as roads and parking lots. From these surfaces, water runs into manufactured diversions that create our stormwater network. This diverted water carries with it the refuse of our automobile lifestyle such as heavy metals, oils and toxins as well as pet wastes and other chemicals applied to the land surface. Stormwater travels through culverts, drainage ditches and retention ponds, eventually soaking into the ground or traveling to tributaries of rivers and into lakes and offshore dumps. Stormwater runoff is one of the greatest environmental threats to our aquifer and one that requires the largest investment in infrastructure.

Golf Courses and Sports Facilities

Golf courses and sport facilities are often over-manicured, colored and treated with harmful chemicals. These areas may serve as recharge zones, but if they carry contaminants into the groundwater, they negate their value as green space. Some courses have developed higher standards, such as Audubon International certification. These courses use native plant species, drought-tolerant turf and water conservation measures that have a lower impact on the aquifer and springs.

Cave Terminology

Cave divers use a variety of words to describe the passages through which they swim.

Phreatic - Refers to submerged cave conduits that were formed and/or enlarged below the water table. Water action over the rock as well as chemical dissolution contributes to the formation of phreatic tubes. Carved scallops in the rock

Stalactites are initially formed in a dry cave, when water soaks through the earth and drips from the ceiling in an air filled passage. Photo by Jill Heinerth.

are a sign indicating water flow and phreatic activity.

Vadose - Refers to cave passages or spaces that are formed above the water table. Flowing streams as well as atmospheric, chemical dissolution or deposition may cause the enlargement process. Delicate speleothems found in submerged Mexican caves were formed when the passage was dry. These decorations are evidence of vadose formation.

Caves that were formed vadose can be later filled with water under higher global sea levels. Caves such as this one have been dry at least times in the last 350,000 years. Photo of the Badlands in Abaco by Jill Heinerth.

Breakdown - Refers to a room containing a boulder pile or slope of debris, which likely crumbled from the ceiling at one time in its development.

Spring - A cave opening or vent from which water is flowing.

Head Pool/Head Spring - The basin of water at the entrance of a cave or spring. This is also known as a spring vent, spring basin, or simply, basin.

Spring Run - The small stream leading from the spring entrance to another water body such as a river.

Siphon - A cave opening into which water flows, downstream. These are also known as ponors, go-away holes, insurgences, sucks, sinks, syphons, swallets and estavelles. Siphons are sometimes characterized by a circular pattern of moving water on the surface. A local accumulation of debris may be present as well as actual disappearance of debris into the hole.

Karst Window - This is a term that refers to a spring/siphon complex. In this configuration, upstream and downstream flows are both present in a pool. Water enters the pool from below ground, crosses the opening and descends again downstream. These may also be referred to as flowing sinks or insurgence/resurgence systems. Karst windows may be associated with rising and sinking streams like the Santa Fe River in Florida. They may be observed in many diving locations including Florida's popular, Wes Skiles Peacock Springs State Park.

This siphon is draining vast quantities of stormwater underground into the Rose Creek System in North Florida. Siphons can also occur in an even more transient presentation in tidal Blue Holes. Some siphons can be extremely dangerous and local guidance is advised before planning a dive in an inflowing cave. Photo: Jill Heinerth

Sinkhole - A typical sinkhole is often the shape of an hourglass, containing a debris mound, known as a talus cone, at the bottom. They may be formed gradually or suddenly, and are found worldwide. Sinkholes may be caused by gradual dissolution from percolating water and subsequent collapse of the cave roof. They may be formed after a lowering of the water table or during flood periods that wash away critical underground support structures. New sinkholes are sometimes human-induced by over pumping of groundwater, removal of tree cover, or modification of natural drainage patterns.

Dr. Kenny Broad prepares a rope to enter Owl Hole on the island of Abaco in the Bahamas. Photo: Jill Heinerth

In other parts of the world, sinkholes may be referred to by different names. Mexicans refer to sinkholes as cenotes. Citizens of the Dominican Republic call them pozos and Bahamians call them Blue Holes. Sinkholes, also known as sinks, may be as small as a foot wide or large enough to swallow a city block.

In May 1981, during a significant drought, a massive sinkhole opened up in Winter Park, Florida. In a single day, the hole widened to over 300 feet (95 m) and to a depth of almost 100 feet (30 m), swallowing a car dealership, swimming pool and large portions of roadway.

Sinkholes are not necessarily found above the water table. The entrances can also be submerged beneath fresh and saltwater environments. Photo: Jill Heinerth

Offset Sink - A sinkhole, which still retains base level flow from either an upstream or downstream direction. An example of this type of sink is Orange Grove in Luraville, Florida.

58

Caletta - A term used in Mexico that refers to the location where a freshwater spring empties into a coastal lagoon. Ya Kul Lagoon in Akumal, Mexico is a good example of this type of geology. Dozens of freshwater vents spill into this large lagoon.

Sump - A water-filled section of a cave that rises and terminates an air-filled passage of a cave.

Sump Diving - The type of cave diving that couples dry caving with diving. It is one of the most advanced and remote forms of the sport.

Sump diving can be one of the most dangerous forms of caving. Getting the equipment to the dive entry can be treacherous and requires an abundance of experience and caution. Photo of Whip Cave on Christmas Island by Jill Heinerth.

Underground Lake - A large lake within an air-filled cave passage.

Speleothems - Delicate carbonate formations on the ceilings and floors of caves, which were formed by dripping water when the cave was previously dry. Columns, stalactites (ceiling), stalagmites (floors), helictites (formed with wind), rim pools, shields, bacon strips and pearls are examples of types of speleothems. If broken, these formations are gone forever.

Speleothems can be easily broken. If you stay on the guideline, you will minimize the impact caused by your bubbles. Like a trail in a National Park, guidelines keep all divers on the same path through the environment. Photo of Dan's Cave in Abaco, Bahamas by Jill Heinerth.

Environmental Hazards in Caves

Some people have referred to cave diving as the world's most dangerous sport, largely because of their perception of environmental hazards. Every crisis that you face underwater must be managed within the overhead setting, with possibly significant delay before exit. The ceiling prevents direct ascent. Passages may be small, complicated and certainly void of light. Emergencies may occur at great penetrations. Added up, these hazards can create stress and task loading. With proper training, awareness and referencing skills, these general risks can be mitigated. Other, specific risks vary from cave to cave.

Visibility

On any given day, visibility may vary greatly due to environmental factors such as runoff, flooding and seasonal fluctuations. As divers, we also have an enormous influence on the visibility within cave systems. Caves contain a variety of substrates. Some caves are composed of hard rock; others, softer, more easily damaged substrate. Gypsum caves vary from limestone, which differs from dolomite. The sediments within the cave affect visibility and may include: sand, silt, clay, mud, organic matter, bacterial growth, algal colonies and marine organisms.

Kristine Rae Olmsted emerges from a silty cave passage.
Photo: Jill Heinerth

When divers disturb the substrate or sediment, it is referred to as silting. Simply passing through a tunnel may knock silt off of a wall, while bubbles tend to form percolation that hits the ceiling of a cave. The greatest negative impact can be caused by poor propulsion techniques. Bad fin technique; "fly-swatting" with hands, poorly stowed equipment dragging on the bottom and lack of buoyancy control will all cause silting.

The worst type of silt tends to be clay. As the lightest sediment particle, it may stay suspended in the water column longer than anything else. Low flow caves that have been "silted-out" may take hours, days or weeks to clear. High flow systems usually flush out much faster.

Chemicals and Water Quality

Besides sediment, divers may come across various chemical compositions that affect visibility. Tannic acid is a basic ingredient in the chemical staining of wood. Tannins are naturally present in woods like oak, walnut, and cypress. These trees leach their stain into rivers such as the Suwannee and Santa Fe, turning them a tea-like shade of red. Tannic acid may be encountered in river caves and may seep into other caves through ceiling cracks. Tannic acid may also be trapped above the clear water in a ceiling dome of a cave for a long period of time.

Hydrogen sulfide is the chemical compound with the formula H_2S. It is partially responsible for the foul odor of rotten eggs and flatulence. This colorless, flammable gas is a byproduct of bacterial breakdown in the absence of oxygen and occurs in sewers and swamps, sinkholes, volcanoes and some water wells. Underwater, it tends to occupy a specific layer and often appears as a white, milky zone. As the diver penetrates this layer, they will notice the sulfurous odor and may experience symptoms of watery eyes or tingling facial skin in high concentrations. Although a diver will rarely meet with high enough concentrations to cause illness, contact with hydrogen sulphide should be minimized.

In some other instances, water becomes stratified in layers that disturb normal vision. When freshwater sits on top of saltwater, as witnessed in some Mexican caves, the meeting zone is called a halocline. When a diver reaches a halocline, they will not only experience a buoyancy change, but may also have difficulty focusing their eyes in the mixing water. Chemical and biological cave formation tends to be very active at the level of the halocline and as a result, you may be in a position where you must swim through the halocline for long distances. In this case, careful contact with the guideline is advised. The freshwater lens and saltwater depths are influenced by various sources, so visibility may vary greatly in the different layers. Stratified water temperatures may create thermoclines, which sometimes disturb visibility.

Seasonal algae blooms may also affect visibility in the entrance of caves. Warm summer weather often heats up the basin of a sinkhole causing a loss of visibility in the shallow areas. Ordinarily, once the diver reaches the flowing spring water, they will find improved visibility.

Current

Flow may have the single greatest effect on visibility within the cave. High flow may create significant resistance to entering a cave, but will assist in a

This screen capture from the film Water's Journey – Hidden Rivers of Florida shows the author struggling through dynamic flow in a restriction. Flow can be strong enough to prevent a diver from entering. Wes Skiles.

speedy exit. By referencing the cave morphology, divers can choose the path of least resistance. Much like shielding your body behind the bulkhead of a wreck or behind a large reef spur, divers can learn to work smartly in high flow scenarios. Flow tends to be the highest where large volumes of water are forced through small openings and restrictions. The flow sculpts scallops in the rock and ripples in the sand and those signs may be used to find the best places to travel through. In high flow, buoyancy changes may not be noticed and need be anticipated when the flow subsides.

Low flow caves have their own unique hazards. The outbound trip will take at least as long as the inbound trip, so careful gas management will be important. Passages tend to be more silt laden and the particulate will not be flushed away. Whatever is disturbed on the way in, will need to be dealt with on the return trip. Systems with absolutely no flow are extremely vulnerable to silting. Particles of silt may stay suspended for long periods.

In lower flow caves, the silt can be stirred up and then hangs in the water column. It can take hours or even weeks to settle. Photo of Paul Heinerth diving in Bermuda by Jill Heinerth.

Downstream flow in siphons can be very dangerous to inexperienced cave divers. Gas management must be calculated to include a longer trip out of the cave. Downstream siphons tend to contain more silt because surface sediments are regularly swept into the cave. Any debris or silt that is stirred up when entering a cave will travel with the team throughout their penetration.

62

Tides are another source of flow in cave systems. In some regions, such as the Bahamas, dives must be carefully planned to account for tidal currents, which can be completely unmanageable during certain times of the day. Local knowledge is critical for diving caves with tidal influence. Within a 24-hour timeframe, there may be only two short windows of opportunity for diving. In general, divers arrive on site in time to witness the ebbing of the inflowing tide. They enter the cave at end of that inflow. Diving is conducted through the slack tide and the beginning of the outflow. Current carries the diver back to the entrance as the flow increases. Tides within caves are tricky and don't always coincide with local charts. Observation and conservatism are critical. Mistimed dives can result in a diver being trapped by flow, pinned to coral on exit or blown off of decompression. Some Bahamian cave vents have epic cultural histories. At Lusca's Breath, offshore Andros, a whirling vortex marks the opening on inflowing tides. Local Bahamians have rumored of lost boats, sea monsters and other dangers in these regions.

Restrictions

Restrictions force a team into a single file. These small spaces may be silty and could make air sharing and line-laying difficult. In some restrictions, a poorly laid line may result in significant delays or entanglement that trap a diver on the bad side of the restriction. A television producer once noted to me, "One second you're a valued member of a cave-diving team. In the next, you're the cork in the bottle containing the lives of your friends." These small spaces should be avoided by anyone other than highly experienced, qualified cave divers with a careful eye for risk assessment.

When it comes time to turn a dive and head for home, it is important to select a spot where the entire team can safely turn around without having an impact on the cave or visibility. Restrictions and other small spaces may not be suitable for turning around and should be avoided when you get close to the time you want to call the dive.

Navigation

Some caves are very linear and others branch out in dendritic conduits like tree branches. Complex cave systems create navigational hazards that should be carefully assessed. In addition to maintaining a continuous guideline, prudent cave divers carefully reference natural formations as they swim through a cave and take time to back-reference the appearance of passages behind them. Everything looks different on the way out of a cave, so penetrations should be limited to distances that can be sufficiently referenced by the diver.

Air Pockets

If you find an air space within a cave, never assume that it is breathable. It may contain low levels of oxygen, high levels of carbon dioxide or other substances such as methane gas. Some air pockets are caused by trapped air from diver exhaust. In other locations, air pockets may indicate that you have risen above the water table. But, organic gases, which are not safe to breathe, may also create air pockets. Some dry pockets above the water table may be filled with bat guano and possible exposure to histoplasmosis. Histoplasma capsula-

You may break the surface during a cave dive, but do not assume the air will be breathable. Photo shot in La Sirena cave in the Dominican Republic by Jill Heinerth.

tum is a fungus which grows in soil and material contaminated with bird or bat droppings. If you ascend into an air pocket, you should leave your mask on and continue to breathe from your regulator unless you are certain that the space is safe. In some locations in Florida and Mexico, safe air pockets within the

cave are marked with a "T" or a short jump and a line arrow that is marked "AIR." These emergency bailout chambers are marked to assist divers in finding a safe place to surface, breathe and talk. However, divers spending time in small air pockets may deplete oxygen levels and increase carbon dioxide to dangerous levels. If you feel odd, air-starved, or are hyperventilating, immediately return to your regulator and breathe from your tank.

CONSERVATION
LANDOWNERS

CHAPTER 6

Conservation and Landowner Relationships

Geology

Conservation includes protecting fragile formations within caves. These formations may include delicate rock, colorful layers of clay or speleothems. Some of these formations may have taken many thousands of years to form and may have been created during much earlier geologic epochs. A stalagmite recovered from Dan's Cave in Abaco was studied and dated by Dr. Peter Swart at University of Miami who confirmed the rock formation to be over three hundred and fifty thousand years old. Such information is not only interesting but provides a glimpse of what the earth was like during very different times. Climatologists are using this data to reconstruct ice ages and dry periods. Red Saharan dust layered within the rock in Abaco's caves tell of a time when vast quantities of particulate traveled across the Atlantic to paint a colorful film on the Bahamian islands.

Biology

Caves are hardly lifeless realms of darkness. They are filled with intriguing, rare life forms, some that are yet be discovered and catalogued for the first time in history. A trogloxene is a species, which uses caves, but cannot complete its life cycle entirely in caves. Troglophiles may complete a life cycle in caves but are also widely known outside of caves. Troglobites are adapted to caves and live their entire life cycle in caves. Stygobites are aquatic troglobites.

Stygobitic cave animals have a unique survival strategy. Living in subaquatic darkness, these creatures have enhanced senses of smell, taste and vibration detection. Eyes and pigment, and other unused anatomical features gradually disappeared. These animals are often endemic to a single, remote site, adapting to its particular environment and very scarce food sources. Many cave animals are basically living fossils, having remained unchanged for many tens of millions of years. As essential missing links, they help scientists better understand the origins of life in our oceans and early roots of life on earth. Cave animals give us a glimpse into history and are an indicator of stability in an ecosystem. As we learn more about these unique creatures, we may learn about evolution and adaptability in a changing world.

Dr. Tom Iliffe examines a small cave adapted crustacean from Sawmill Sink in the Bahamas. Photo: Jill Heinerth

Cave Fauna

Scientists and bio-prospectors are interested in the life found inside caves. Many organisms inside caves live chemosynthetically rather than photosynthetically. Some of the substances gleaned from caves contain chemicals and materials that interest medical researchers, the pharmaceutical industry and chemical companies. Researchers in the Bahamas have discovered anti-bacterial and anti-cancer agents within sponges inside caves. These sponges apparently contain more potent compounds than their open ocean relatives. Conservation of water quality may be critical to protecting the habitat of these organisms.

Cave divers may impact organisms in many ways. Environmental damage may disturb habitat. Bubbles may dislodge animals and even change water chemistry. Lights brought from the open water to the entrance of a cave may attract open water animals to feast on a new buffet of animals in areas that were previously darkened. Some caves have been closed completely for the purpose of conservation, or limited to rebreather-only diving for protection.

Remipede from Dan's Cave in Abaco. Photo: Jill Heinerth

67

Bacterial Colonies and Algal Mats

Even less is known about the significance of bacterial colonies and algal mats in caves. Because these colonies live chemosynthetically, they are of great interest to astro-biologists. This type of life takes many forms. In Florida, I have swum through virgin caves that are draped with what I call "snotcicles." In other regions, I have seen interesting white films seeping out of cracks in the rocks. I once saw a large, basketball-sized, translucent orb float out of a small outflowing tunnel followed by other smaller gelatinous globes. In Otter Spring, in Florida, golf ball-sized, orange jelly masses tumble into standing waves sculpted by the flow. In Cherokee Road Extension Cave in Abaco, thick orange mats with rust-colored, porous tendrils reach up through the halocline. Witnessing these forms of life is a privilege, but they are delicate and should be preserved.

Cultural Artifacts

Conservation includes protecting cultural and paleontological artifacts and specimens. In many cultures, caves are thought of as gateways to the underworld and carry great significance to local inhabitants. Artifacts and even humans were sacrificed in caves around the world. Indigenous peoples may still feel connected to these portals as resting places for their ancestors. Archaeologists rely on artifacts remaining undisturbed in order to gather accurate data.

Work is currently underway to catalog and digitally preserve artifacts in caves around the world. The National Geographic sponsored Digital Preservation Project spearheaded by engineer and cave diver Corey Jaskolski (www.DigitalPreservation.org) conducts highly detailed scanning in situ and then builds very high resolution models of sensitive artifacts and paleontological remains. These data can be examined by scientists or can be used in outreach activities with virtual reality and augmented reality devices such as the Microsoft Hololens.

A local Mayan guide interacts with augmented reality (AR) images of cultural remains through a headset. He is able to see 3D rendered items within the context of his surroundings. Photo: Jill Heinerth

68

Brian Kakuk recovers the skull of a Lucayan Indian from Stargate cave in Andros, Bahamas. The skull was examined by Michael Pateman for the Bahamas Museum of Natural History. Photo from the National Geographic Society project examining the blue holes of the Bahamas by Jill Heinerth.

Traffic

Divers should always try to stay close to permanent guidelines in the cave. It is much like following a trail through a national park. By following the guideline trail, your damage will be either minimized or localized. In places where delicate ceiling formations are present, this is xtremely important. Mere bubbles from your regulator can permanently dislodge and destroy delicate formations such as soda straws. Careless or needless pulling can tumble stalagmites off of their base. Where possible, divers should avoid physical contact with any part of the cave.

Mitigation

Good buoyancy skills, proper fin technique, appropriate gear choice and configuration contribute to protecting the cave. Pulling through the cave should be limited to high flow systems where gliding against the flow is impossible. Contact with cave animals should be avoided and care should be taken to avoid luring open water fish into the cave. In these cases, leaving your light off through the cavern zone may help. Keeping cave sites cleared of trash and debris are responsibilities of cave divers; since anything discarded topside may end up in the cave through carelessness, stormwater runoff or flooding. Collecting anything from a cave should be restricted to scientists with a permit, and divers should not support the trade or display of minerals, speleothems, rocks, cultural artifacts or biological materials.

Turning the Tables

In the early days of our sport, cave divers were perceived as adrenaline junkies who were both foolhardy and inconsiderate. In the past, legislators have been on the verge of closing sites and completely outlawing the sport. Over a period of several decades, that image has been overturned to the point where cave divers are being recognized for making significant contributions to science and conservation. Focusing attention on water conservation, many cave divers have become involved in protection groups and have brought environmental concerns to the forefront of governmental interests and the media. Cave scientists work in the fields of hydrology, biology, archaeology, and other areas. By these involvements, the sport has become elevated and access to many sites has been assured.

Landowner Relations

Whether you are a scientific or recreational cave diver, good relationships with landowners are critical. In the past, divers sneaking onto private property have fostered waves of discontent. It is imperative that you seek permission to enter private land. Trespassing could land you in jail and may also result in site closure for other divers. Access privileges are tenuous in a litigious world. Care should be taken to follow established rules and ensure that the landowner has a good experience with everyone that visits their property.

Federal and state lands, including parks and preserves, usually have strict access policies. In Florida, some parks require the diver to surrender their certification card prior to park entry and collect it at an agreed upon time later in the day. Other locations have developed specific timeframes for diving. In Australia, many systems are open only to guided diving or online bookings. In Finland, mine diving is regulated through an event-booking system. These procedures were established to protect landowners, enhance safety and ensure that the carrying capacity for a site is never exceeded.

Cave divers are role models for other divers at sites where recreational diving and cave diving mix. Answering the questions of inquiring tourists promotes a good reputation for the sport. Gentle correction of recreational divers to keep them out of harm's way is also important. If an open water diver is entering a cave without training or proper equipment, try to resolve the situation and let them know why their actions could result in bad examples, injury or death. Be good stewards of the environment and ambassadors of our sport, by talking with locals, providing information and education, and being respectful of property-owners' rights.

70

EQUIPMENT FOR CAVE DIVING

CHAPTER 7

Equipment for Cave Diving ---------------------

Cave diving requires a tremendous amount of equipment to be conducted safely. The primary goals for selecting equipment should always reflect adequate redundancy with maximum streamlining and simplicity. In other words, a diver should carry just enough gear to handle emergencies that may arise, but not so much that simplicity and good trim are compromised.

The gear that a cave diver wears is their tool kit. If a cave diver also participates in other types of diving, it is desirable to configure the gear in a way that works for the many anticipated environments and activities. If a diver's reel can always be found on the same hip, or if stage bottles are always clipped in the same manner, whether in a cave or on a wreck, the diver will have a better opportunity to react with learned muscle behaviors in a state of emergency.

Given the variety of types of diving and environmental conditions worldwide, there is no perfect gear configuration, only a gear configuration that works for a diver's particular body type, size and surroundings.

Every cave diver should be equipped with the minimum gear described in this chapter.

Cave diver Dr. Darrin York is well equipped as a sidemount cave diver. Photo: Jill Heinerth

Air Supply

Cavern Divers may use single scuba cylinders for venturing within the day-light zone, but beyond the reach of sunlight, divers need either a single cylin-der with a dual-outlet valve (H- or Y-valve) or double tank configurations as described below.

Single tanks should have a minimum starting volume of 70 cft. and twin-diving cylinders should have a minimum starting volume of 140 cft./1980 L. Most cave divers in North America are trained using backmounted double tanks with an isolator manifold, although some argue that using a manifold lacking an isolator actually minimizes failure points. Any manifold that con-nects backmounted cylinders can be a weak link if a diver hits the ceiling of the cave hard enough.

British divers have a lengthier history with sidemount diving configurations, where independent tanks are attached to a harness and hang parallel with the diver's body, beneath the armpits. In the last decade, North American manu-facturers have introduced numerous excellent sidemount rigs that are ex-tremely popular, shifting their emphasis from exploration applications to sheer comfort. Whether you are an explorer or enthusiast, this is likely the largest growing activity within cave diving today.

DIN valve outlets are preferred over standard yokes, because they trap the O-ring seal safely inside the valve. The 200-bar outlet is the most versatile valve style since a small "donut" insert can quickly convert a tank to a standard yoke outlet. 300-bar valves are more secure but cannot be used with donut inserts.

Most cave divers prefer steel cylinders to aluminum tanks since their nega-tive buoyancy negates or lessens the need for a weight belt. Given the option, it is always preferable to carry ballast as air supply in a tank, rather than lead on your body. In tropical environments where little exposure protection is re-quired, aluminum tanks are still very popular.

New divers often purchase unnecessarily large diving cylinders, assuming that more volume is better. It is important to consider that the additional effort needed to swim large tanks through the cave may use up the extra gas supply. Walking with large doubles and lugging them in and out of vehicles and fill stations might also shorten a diver's active career! Additionally, dive turn times will be calculated based on the smallest volume twinset in a group. If your partner has small tanks, you'll be lugging big tanks without gaining the benefit of increased penetration distances. Finally, there is no truth to "one size fits all" when it comes to tanks. It is not reasonable to ask a small person to carry unreasonably large tanks in relation to their body morphology. It is often easier to carry stage bottles in addition to a suitably sized set of double tanks than carry something that is too big or too negative for a small person's frame.

Etienne Mackenson wears a typical double tank set for cave diving. Photo: Jill Heinerth

Mask

Cave divers prefer low-profile masks that are streamlined in high-flow caves. Black mask skirts are popular since they minimize glare caused by the light from a following diver. Neoprene/Velcro mask straps minimize snag potential, but divers with standard straps can reverse the straps or tape them down with electrical tape to eliminate locations that can hook a guideline.

Many cave divers carry a spare mask in a waist pouch or drysuit pocket. These spare masks must be properly inspected and prepped before diving so that they are clear and free of fog when needed. When making a decision about whether to carry a spare mask, temperature and salinity play a key role.

Fins

Simple but powerful fins should be selected with consideration of where the guideline could become snagged. Spring straps are popular for this reason as well as for ease of donning and removal. Standard strap and buckle configurations can be reversed taped or covered with narrow bicycle tire tubing to minimize catch points.

Careful thought should be given to the selection of fins with appropriate buoyancy characteristics. Some divers will find that the popular "Jet Fin" design is too negatively buoyant and contributes to silting. Others may find that heavy fins help them deal with positive buoyancy of their drysuit boots. Overly long fins are discouraged since they may cause silting and damage to the walls in small tunnels.

Most cave divers choose spring heel straps rather than buckles. These straps are easy to don and secure and have fewer snag points than standard fin straps. Photo: Jill Heinerth

Buoyancy System

Backmounted "wings" are standard flotation gear for double tanks. Wings come in many varieties and lift capacities. Divers should find a balance between streamlining and adequate lift. There are many different features, beyond lift capacity, that should be considered. Some wings are designed with 360-degree unrestrained airflow path, while others trap gas under bungees or in one lobe. Low-profile elbows on the inflator mechanism are preferred and rear-dump valves should be easy to reach and use in horizontal trim.

Divers using drysuits can use their exposure suit as a source of redundant buoyancy in the event of a wing failure. Wetsuit-clad divers should not get in the water without redundant buoyancy. Before the availability of dual-bladder wings, divers often stacked a second wing on their bolts. Now, several manufacturers make excellent dual-bladder products where the twin cells are encased in a single outer sleeve with two separate inflator mechanisms. Most divers choose to leave the second inflator disconnected and reserve its use for emergency purposes only. Care should be taken to test the function of this wing before diving in case it is needed.

Harness System

The most common harness systems are composed of a backplate with webbing. Backplates may be constructed of stainless steel, aluminum or ABS composite materials. Divers can select the best material based on their buoyancy requirements. Stainless plates are very popular because they are durable and negatively buoyant. However, aluminum and ABS plates are lighter for travel and less negatively buoyant for people that use lighter exposure protection.

Harnesses are often threaded with a single piece of nylon webbing, reducing potential failure points. Deluxe harnesses feature additional rings and quick releases that improve comfort and facilitate easy removal. Some manufacturers have designed single-piece-webbed harnesses that can easily expand and cinch to aid in dressing and removal.

Harnesses are customized with D-rings for hanging stage bottles and accessory gear. Short lengths of bicycle tire inner tube can be used to protect friction points and to provide snug tie-downs for gear that might otherwise dangle from the diver's rig.

Soft harnesses are also gaining popularity with divers who use double tanks. The Dive Rite TransPac was the first soft harness on the market. Designed to provide a more customized fit and padded comfort, many divers feel that this type of design also allows for more comfortable walking to and from the entry point. Hybrid units that combine a hard plate and softly padded ergonomics are also extremely popular.

Gas Delivery

Divers with backmounted doubles need two first-stage regulators, each equipped with a single second-stage. One regulator must be equipped with a minimum, 7-foot hose (5-foot for cavern diving is adequate), to ease air sharing in single-file formation. DPV divers use even longer second-stage hoses to facilitate air sharing while underway.

A doubles diver installs one submersible pressure gauge, a power inflator for the wing(s), and may also have an additional power inflator for their drysuit or redundant wing. Consoles are considered too bulky and are not recommended. Gauges that require air transmitters are discouraged on back mounted tanks unless they can be angled in a way that protects these sensitive items from contact with the cave ceiling and subsequent damage.

There are many differing philosophies on the organization of the two regulators and their accessory hoses, but the key principles are to be streamlined and provide the best redundancy for any possible emergency scenarios that might arise. Extra care must be taken to ensure that hoses to do not stick up above the profile of the first stage in a way that could impact the ceiling of the cave. Hoses should be routed downward for maximum protection and should not loop out sideways from the diver's body in a way that could create a snag hazard.

Many technical divers prefer balanced, downstream regulators. High-performance regulators are available in both piston and diaphragm styles. Cold-water divers often select environmentally sealed, diaphragm first-stages. DIN-style connections are preferred over yokes, since they are more secure and can tolerate higher tanks pressures. Port location and first-stage swivels will affect how hoses may route from the manifold. Keeping hoses well organized will increase their longevity and provide for the best streamlining and ease of deployment.

The majority of backmount cave divers choose to breathe from the long hose, since an out-of-air diver is likely to reach for the one in their mouth first. The long hose is generally wrapped under a right, hip-mounted, light canister. It crosses the waistline, passes behind the left shoulder and drapes on top of the right clavicle to the mouth. This hose must lie on top of all other hoses so that it deploys properly during drills and emergencies.

Exposure Suits

A great majority of cave divers practice their craft in drysuits because of the long duration of their dives. Divers should look for the following features in a drysuit:

- appropriate thermal protection (made up of a combination of the outer suit and engineered undergarments)

- appropriate buoyancy characteristics (neoprene suits are very buoyant and may require adding weight; membrane suits are neutrally buoyant)

- response to flooding (a neoprene suit will maintain some thermal protection in cold water, if flooded, where a membrane suit will not unless it is worn with purpose-built performance undergarments)

- ease of releasing air on ascent in confined spaces

- accessories such as pockets

- fit, streamlining, durability and maneuverability

- seal design that will accommodate active motion without seepage

- footwear design that is conducive to hiking/walking with heavy gear

Accessories such as gaiters and rubber foot restraints will aid in preventing excess air from trapping in the diver's boots.

Undergarment choice is as important as the suit itself for providing good thermal protection. Cotton should never be worn next to the skin. Modern wicking fabrics keep divers drier, and therefore warmer, over long durations. Some engineered undergarments retain thermal capacity when flooded.

Wetsuits are used by divers in warmer climates and by people who dive in tight spaces. Since wetsuits compress and lose buoyancy and thermal capacity at depth, they are generally not preferred for deep diving.

Heating units have been developed for both dry and wetsuit divers. These units are fueled by battery units, exterior to the suit, which are connected through a plug, often located in the drysuit inflator valve. For reasons of safety, batteries should remain outside the suit. Complete heating systems are available from companies such a Santi Diving who have designed a comprehensive group of products that includes fully heated suits, heated vests and even heated gloves. Not to be left out, heated shirts are also available for wetsuit divers. Wetsuit heater batteries are properly designed and sealed to guard against electrocution. Heated undergarments available for other uses are generally not safe for cave diving. As an example, many heated motorcycle vests are inexpensive but may not tolerate flooding. Numerous cave divers have been electrocuted or burned by these and other untested devices.

Much research is currently underway regarding body temperature and decompression stress. Don't be misled to believe that toasty warm is necessarily safe. Warm divers may take on inert gas faster than cool divers and if your heating runs out on decompression, then you may not offgas at an equal ratio. Stay current with developing to research so you can make safe choices about how you use artificial heat during a dive.

Lights

The primary dive light should have an appropriate intensity and burn time that exceeds the dive plan. Many divers select a dive light that has a burn time that is equivalent to at least one-and-a-half times the planned dive, but it makes even more sense to have a rechargeable light that will easily take you through a full day of diving activities. A primary light is usually equipped with a canister-style battery and cord, though recently, the release of lights such as Light & Motion's Sola Tech600 and Halcyon's EON light, mean that divers can now have brilliant performance and longevity without a battery canister. The light head should have a clip, to stow it when not in use, and some sort of handle such as a soft elastic mount or Goodman handle. Popular contemporary primary lights have LED or HID type bulbs. The most modern versions have several power settings to permit diver's to save power when required.

Specifications are hard to interpret between different brands of lights. Claimed specifications often do not match actual performance in the field. You should review: lumens, duration, beam quality, coverage, burn curve, weight/size/buoyancy, depth rating, build quality, company reputation and environmental impact before investing in a light.

Lumens: The lumen is the unit that scientists use to examine the luminous flux from a light source. In essence, lumens, or lumina, accurately describe how bright a light is. The National Institute of Standards and Technology measure lumen output using a device called an integration sphere. They use photometers to count light particles inside the sphere.

In 2009, the American National Standards Institute (ANSI) approved a standard for flashlight performance. The resulting specification called ANSI/NEMA FL-1 is designed to help consumers make fair comparisons of lights and to eliminate exaggerated light performance by quoting odd features such as "emitter lumens" or "out-the-front lumens." The manufacturer or an independent lab can perform the tests, however, the necessary equipment and calibration makes this an expensive undertaking. Few manufacturers test to this standard and share results with consumers. Light & Motion tested many popular brands in comparison to their lights and reports comparative test results on their website at *www.LightandMotion.com.*

Duration and Burn Curve: When lumens are tested, the actual runtime should also be reported. Burn time is determined when the light output drops to 10% of its original value using the batteries included with the light. When viewing the test results of competitive light brands on Light & Motion's website, it appears that numerous manufacturers are over reporting the intensity and burn time. Some models actually performed at 50% of the claimed specification. None of the lights they tested performed better than their advertised quality when tested to the FL-1 standard. It is also interesting to view burn curves to determine whether a light maintains brightness over the duration or whether it quickly lowers intensity to lengthen burn time.

Beam Quality and Coverage: A lighting manufacturer usually specifies whether a light is a "spot" or a "flood" and should indicate how many degrees of coverage the device will deliver. Some lights have an adjustable beam or several power settings that change the focus of the beam. Most cave divers prefer spot coverage, where videographers looks for diffused wide beam coverage.

Weight, Size and Buoyancy: I have often struggled with American airport security, the TSA, when trying to fly with large battery packs and cinema lights. There is a limit to the size of lithium batteries that are allowed on a commercial aircraft. Smaller, lighter units can be easily flown without challenge from airport security. Buoyancy characteristics are also important. Negatively buoyant light heads can be problematic and tiring to swim for any length of time.

Company Reputation: Like all your technical diving equipment, a primary light is an investment and it may need service in the future. Buying lights that are made as close to home as possible from a reputable company makes sense. As with all equipment, customer service, reputation, innovation and warranty are all issues to explore.

Environmental Impact: There are many way that a manufacturer can be environmentally responsible. Using recycled materials, rechargeable batteries and a local workforce will all reduce the environmental impact. If the light has rechargeable batteries it may save significant money over the life of the product. Consider the operating cost and the environment, in your purchase decision.

Backup Lights

Each diver must carry a minimum of two backup diving lights. New LED technology has introduced much longer potential burn times, but each light should be capable of burning the entire dive time. Many divers fuel backup lights with disposable batteries since replaceable rechargeables need more maintenance. Additionally, rechargeable batteries have a steep discharge curve, where disposable alkaline batteries tend to dim for a long period before completely burning out. However, the environmental impact and operating cost of disposable batteries is significant and newer lights with built-in rechargeable batteries and "fuel gauges" are very reliable.

Backup lights are small and streamlined so that they can be easily stowed on the harness or stashed in a thigh pocket. They should have a small clip and be restrained close to the harness or clipped on a tether in a suit pocket. They should never be allowed to dangle freely.

Reels

Cave diving reels are made by several manufacturers in various styles. Key features of a cave diving reel include: a handle that allows the diver to hold a light and deploy line with one hand, a clip for securing to the diver's harness, a lock-down nut that prevents accidental deployment of line and a spool with winding knob.

Each team carries one primary cave-diving reel with minimum 350 feet/110 meters of guideline to connect the open water with the main line inside the cave. Each diver must also carry at least one safety reel/spool with a minimum of 100 feet/30 meters of guideline (larger for some very big caves). This reel or spool will be used to search for

A side-winding primary reel. Note the diver uses his finger as a brake to prevent the reel from unspooling too fast. Photo: Jill Heinerth

lost divers, a lost guideline or to patch a broken line within the cave. It is very common to carry a second safety reel or more commonly a safety spool.

Jump/gap reels or spools are used to bridge the opening from the main line to side passages that are not connected with continuous line. Divers beyond introductory level will carry the number of reels needed for a particular dive plan. These reels typically carry 50 to 100 feet of line.

Most cave diving reels are loaded with double braided nylon line of varying thickness. This line is highly abrasion-resistant and does not float. Permanent guidelines in caves are often made of a material called Kernmantle. An inner, nylon core is sheathed with a strong double-braided casing. Occasionally, polypropylene line is used in marine caves, where biological growth can eat through other lines in short order. Polypro is not easy to deploy because it floats, but it maintains its strength even when coated with organisms, and is sometimes used as a hand line to protect fragile environments.

Information Systems

Each diver needs to carry a dive computer or timing device with depth gauge, a slate or notebook with pencil and submersible dive tables or back-up computer. Caves are multi-level, complex dives, and two computers are preferred over all other methods.

Knives

Knives are used to cut entangled line and to patch damaged or broken line. Knives should be configured to minimize entanglement and be placed on the diver's body so that they can be safely deployed with either hand. Small knives or line cutters are best. Small knives can be mounted on the wrist strap of a dive computer for very easy deployment.

Referencing Exit Markers (REMs) are used as personal markers. Point the large paddle towards your exit. Photo: Courtesy of Apeks.

Markers

Cave divers carry a minimum of three directional markers such as plastic line arrows and numerous non-directional markers called "cookies," or clothespins. Referencing Exit Markers (REMs) are the newest style of personal marker. Directional markers are used to mark jumps or may be used in emergency situations such as losing the line or your buddy. Clothespins and cookies may be used as attendance markers indicating the exit side of a "T" or jump. They can be used for surveys and may mark maximum penetration when planning complex dives such as traverses or circuits. Divers should clearly personalize their markers by consistently writing their initials or name on the face and should find a way to make them unique to touch so they can be differentiated from those of others.

81

Decompression Cylinders

For dives involving decompression, divers place a decompression tank in the cave. The cylinder volume should be adequate to supply twice the gas volume required to complete decompression. These cylinders are usually placed 10 feet deeper than the stop where they will be required. Some cave configurations make it necessary to drop the tank deeper than the gas can be safely used. In this case, the first-stage mouthpiece may be covered with a simple, physical barrier that alerts a diver to the fact that it should not be breathed at its current depth. All cylinders should be properly marked, displaying contents and maximum operating depth (MOD). These markings should be readable by both the diver and buddy. When not in use, regulator hoses should be neatly stowed under an elasticized band on the bottle, with the bottle turned off, but left pressurized.

Decompression tanks and stage bottles can be clipped on a D-ring in the clavicle region and hip, or may be clipped on the hip or butt-plate and secured at the valve area with a bungee that extends from under the diver's armpit. This technique, borrowed from sidemount divers, keeps the cylinders in the most streamlined position, parallel with the diver's side. Stage tanks that are not streamlined can cause cave damage as well as contribute to poor trim. Given that many caves present the diver with the challenge of swimming against the flow and given that stage bottles are carried great distances into the cave, they should be well placed for maximum streamlining.

Gear Configuration

There are many different configurations and philosophies that enable streamlining and good trim. Each piece of equipment must be carefully thought out and stowed appropriately with the following considerations:

Redundancy: A diver should carry precisely enough equipment to deal with foreseeable failures, but nothing additional that could clutter the configuration or reduce effective deployment and operation of necessary gear. Simplicity is paramount.

Streamlining: All equipment should be thoughtfully stowed in a way that maximizes streamlining of the gear and body.

Comfort: Each piece of auxiliary gear should be easy to secure, stow and operate while maintaining horizontal trim. Divers have a range of differing body morphologies and flexibility; therefore solutions may differ slightly from diver to diver.

Consistency: In some cases, consistency will be critical within a project or dive team. Groups like the WKPP have mandated a standard configuration for all of their divers. This may be worth bearing in mind, especially for project-oriented diving, as long as the above tenets are also satisfied.

Cross-Platform Compatibility: If you dive a variety of configurations like backmounted doubles, sidemount, rebreathers and single tanks you should find a configuration that remains consistent from rig to rig. For example, you should always be able to find your backup diving light in the same location. Stage bottles should be secured in the same way from unit to unit. Additionally, if you participate in a variety of types of diving like wreck, cave, ice and others, you should find something that works no matter how many undergarments are worn under your drysuit and no matter how thick your cold-water gloves may be.

The ultimate goal is to work with a given configuration repeatedly, until muscle memory allows the diver to react quickly to secure gear or deal with an emergency.

Single Tank Diving

When training at the levels of Cavern, Introduction to Cave some divers choose to wear a single tank configuration. Although not necessarily required at the cavern level, dual-outlet valves are highly recommended. These types of valves allow the diver to shut down one regulator while still having access to the gas supply from the other regulator. Single tank configurations may be more difficult to trim effectively, since a lot of gear on a single tank may shift around if not fitted well.

Backmounted Doubles

Double, backmounted tanks with an isolator manifold have been the gear of choice for most cave divers for decades. The isolator manifold allows divers to cut off the connection between the two, backmounted tanks. In the event of a burst disk failure, valve or manifold failure of the neck O-ring leak, the center knob can be closed to protect the non-affected side from dumping. In this case, the diver continues to breathe the damaged side to use as much escaping gas as possible before switching regulators.

At some destinations such as Mexico, divers may find non-isolator manifolds to be popular rentals. Many operators prefer these because of lower maintenance. Independent, backmounted doubles are rare but used by a few divers, especially travelers that do not have access to manifolds.

In all cases, backmounted tanks should be secured to a harness system with bands, bolts and wing nuts. Soft cam bands are not stable enough to safely mount doubles to a harness system.

Double tanks should be positioned to facilitate horizontal trim. Tank valves must be easily reachable in a horizontal, swimming position, as well as vertically on the surface.

Divers almost universally place their primary, long-hose regulator on the right post of their manifold. If they contact the ceiling and damage the right, valve knob, it will sheer off in a working position that allows the diver to continue breathing. When the left side of the manifold hits the ceiling, it tends to roll into the "off" position. Sheering a valve could leave the valve stuck in an off position, robbing the diver of the ability to breathe from that regulator.

Sidemount

Sidemount diving is one of the fastest growing specialties in the sport. Formerly reserved for explorers, this configuration has been popularized by new gear availability. With sidemounting, the diver carries two, independent cylinders clipped to their harness. The lower end of the tank is clipped on a butt-plate or butterfly D-ring, and the valve is generally looped with a bungee or clipped in a way that it rides in line with the diver's body. In horizontal swimming position, the tanks should align perfectly with the diver and create a very low profile. Some divers embrace this technique for exploring low bedding planes, but many divers enjoy the comfort of the configuration and the ease of carrying a single tank at a time to the filling station or the water's edge.

Numerous manufacturers offer ready-made sidemount units. Buying one of these and getting professional fitting assistance from an experienced instructor shortens an otherwise frustrating learning curve. Gas management skills are critical to ensure adequate tank pressure is available from either tank if there is an emergency.

Sidemount divers tend to consider themselves much more independent in the event

Good sidemount trim is demonstrated by instructors Edmund Yiu and Garry Dallas. Photo by Jill Heinerth

of an emergency than backmount divers. In a gas supply emergency, tank valves are easy to see and operate if a failure occurs. For complete information on sidemount diving, purchase the book "Sidemount Profiles," by Jill Heinerth and Brian Kakuk or view the video "Sidemount Diving." Both are available on www.intoThePlanet.com or on Amazon.

Rebreathers

Rebreather configurations must be as streamlined as open circuit configurations. It is imperative that divers carefully examine the position of bailout cylinders to ensure that they are not damaging the cave. Most cave divers prefer separating their bailout gas into two tanks for redundancy and balance. Divers in mixed teams have many additional planning and safety considerations, which are discussed later in Chapter Ten.

For detailed information on rebreathers, look for the comprehensive text "The Basics of Rebreather Diving" on Amazon.com.

Instructor Trainer Steve Lewis shows streamlined bailout bottles on the Sentinel rebreather. Photo: Jill Heinerth

Problem Solving - Challenges

Are you a survivor? Assemble and don your cave diving gear and sit comfortably on the floor to test your dexterity and problem solving capability with the following challenges:
First-stage, high-pressure-seat failure on right side
Impact with ceiling causes manifold to rupture
Wing is inflating continually
Drysuit is inflating continuously
Second-stage free flow on O_2 bottle
Primary light failure
Passing a "T" in cave
A blown high-pressure hose
SPG is trickling bubbles at the fitting to the HP hose
Pressure gauge is not dropping

Pressure gauge reads zero
Lost mask
Inflator tears off of wing
Wing won't hold gas
Oxygen tank is missing
Turned on drysuit inflation bottle and the hose exploded

It is critically important to recognize that some failures require immediate closure of the isolator valve in the center of a set of manifolded doubles. A manifold rupture could quickly result in the loss of both tanks of gas, but if the isolator is closed quickly, then the remaining contents in one tank may be conserved.

On the other hand, if it is determined that an isolator valve is closed, it may not be prudent to open it during the course of a dive. One should question whether one side could have a different mix than the other. If partial pressure blending techniques were used, it is possible that an unbreathable mix may reside in one tank. At least one cave diving accident has occurred when a diver

lost consciousness after breathing from a hypoxic trimix content after analyzing the other tank and beginning a dive with a closed isolator valve.

Prior to diving, discuss and rehearse solutions to specific risks that might be forthcoming on the dive. Photo: Jill Heinerth

Problem Solving - Solutions

First-stage, high-pressure-seat failure on right side

When a first-stage, high-pressure-seat fails, it will usually result in over-pressurization that heads downstream, causing a second-stage free flow. It can be subtle or dramatic. A slow bubbling from the second-stage that creeps up slowly after a breath indicates a seat failure. A catastrophic failure may sounds like a large bang, followed by a free flow that can be powerful enough to eject the second-stage from the diver's mouth. The bubbles may be momentarily stopped after pressing the purge and releasing pressure that has built up. If the first-stage is not shut down, a hose may rupture. The valve must be shut down if the flow is significant. The diver should switch to their alternate second-stage and think about the other hoses that are coming from that side. Will it affect your drysuit inflator or the wing? Abort the dive and exit while monitoring supplies.

Impact with ceiling causes manifold to rupture

You will need to close the manifold isolator and breathe from the side that is quickly dumping. Use all the escaping air you can before switching to your backup regulator. Be ready to share air as you exit in case you run out. What other features will you lose? Is your pressure gauge attached to the empty side? What about inflation? What about your drysuit? How will this affect your exit strategy or decompression?

Wing is inflating continually

Unplug the inflator hose. You can orally inflate the wing, as needed or use your drysuit or a backup wing for buoyancy. The inflator button might be sticking. The Schrader valve in the hose might be sticking. The first stage may be suffering from a failure of the HP seat. Look for additional symptoms like a free-flow of the second stage.

Drysuit is inflating continuously

Unplug the drysuit inflator hose. If you only need to ascend you may not require any more gas in the drysuit. However, it is smart to switch the wing inflator hose to the drysuit just in case, and use the drysuit for buoyancy. If the wing is required for sufficient lift, you can switch back or orally inflate as needed. Remain vigilant in watching for other failures that might be tied to a failing first stage HP seat.

Second-stage free flow on oxygen bottle

Feather the tank valve on and off for each breath you consume. If this is too difficult, allow your partner to complete their oxygen decompression and take their bottle to finish yours.

Primary light failure

Reference the line and continue to stay with the group while you switch to your backup light. Signal the team and abort the dive, placing you in the middle or front of the group for exit. Do not trail the group, since your backup light may not be powerful enough to be seen, if you signal for assistance.

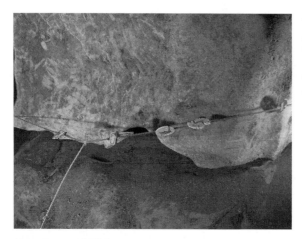

Using personal markers at jumps and Ts can not only inform the team with "attendance markers" but might also advise other teams when a passage is already crowded with a large team of divers. Photo: Jill Heinerth

Passing a "T" in cave

Mark the exit side of the "T" with your own marker. Can you do this neutrally buoyant, while swimming, without losing time?

A blown high-pressure hose

The SPG is the only gear fed by a high-pressure hose. This is actually less catastrophic than a low-pressure hose explosion. The hole in the HP hose is the size of a pinpoint, where a low-pressure hose has a large bore. Gas will dump quicker from a severed low-pressure hose. In either case, you have to close the valve on the offending side (if the gas loss is significant) and switch to a working regulator.

SPG is trickling bubbles from fitting to hose

This is a common failure of one of two O-rings on the swivel fitting in the SPG. A leaking HP hose looks very similar when it leaks at the swivel fitting. These tiny bubbles are often tolerated by divers, reasoning that the leak is minor, but this is a quick repair as long as you have a fresh swivel or two, 003 sized O-rings. Keep them in your kit.

SPG is not dropping

Check to see if your isolator is closed. Check to see if your left valve has impacted the ceiling and rolled off.

The left side of the manifold can turn off when the valve hits the ceiling of the cave. Photo: Jill Heinerth

88

Pressure gauge reads zero

If you are still able to breathe, perhaps your left post has rolled off and the remaining air in the hose has leaked out.

Lost mask

Deploy your spare mask if you have one. Did you prepare it just like your primary mask? Has it been treated with defog or is it a moldy mess in your damp pocket? Alert team members and consider aborting since you are now using gear intended for emergency use.

Inflator tears off of wing

This can happen when the heat-sealing of the bladder fails or when a diver is forced through a restriction in high flow. This represents a total loss of buoyancy. Use your drysuit or switch to your redundant wing, if available.

The rules of accident analysis apply at all times. Smart, experienced divers run reels for all their jumps and never accept a visual jump as a safe diving practice. Photo: Jill Heinerth

Wing won't hold gas

If your wing won't hold gas, it is possible that you have experienced a rupture, but more likely, your pull dump is snagged in the open position or has become blocked open by debris. Sometimes the bead or knot on the end of a pull cord gets caught under the waistband or in a hip D-ring. Find the string or bead and free it. Then attempt to re-inflate.

Oxygen tank is missing

Your decompression plans should include the possibility of your tank being missing, empty or disabled. If you must remain on a leaner deco mix, will your gas supply be adequate to get you through all of your deco? If not, allow your buddy to complete their decompression and then use their remaining gas to finish yours.

Turned on drysuit inflation bottle and the hose exploded

If you failed to install an over-pressure relief valve (OPV) on the first-stage, then a high-pressure-seat failure will cause up to 3000 psi of gas to rush through a hose rated for significantly less. It can explode and render the supply unusable. You can take your wing inflator and plug it into the drysuit valve in order to exit. If you do not have a second-stage on a bottle, or if you have installed inline, shut-off sliders, you must install OPVs on the first-stage as relief for over-pressurization. The bang of an exploded hose is not just loud; it may whip you like a rented mule.

Skills and drills should be practiced both out of the water and in the cave. Proficiency requires practice. Photo: Jill Heinerth

CAVE DIVING
TECHNIQUE

CHAPTER 8

91

Technique --

Technical diving and specifically, cave diving, is a continual learning process. If we closely examine how we learn, we can better prepare for the pitfalls associated with each stage of the learning process.

Gordon Training International is popularly considered to be the originator of the *Conscious Competence Model*, which describes the steps of learning any new skill. This model is particularly applicable to technical diving.

The model describes the first-stage of learning as "unconscious-incompetent" or "unconscious-unskilled." This stage describes a cave diver on the day in double tanks; they are unaware of the proper function their gear and incapable of determining risk. They simply don't know what can kill them.

Stage two, and each stage thereafter, is often associated with a sensation of awakening, when the person feels "like a light bulb went off." As they make a step forward, they enter the realm of "conscious-incompetence." At this point, the diver is beginning to fully comprehend the function and location of their gear and is able to assess risks, but needs close supervision.

Next, the learner reaches the point of "conscious-competence." This may be the point when they complete their initial cave training. At this level, the diver has mastered basic manual skills, has a good assessment of risk and is able to complete self or buddy-rescue. This may indeed be the moment where they are the safest technical diver they can be. They still have a healthy fear that keeps them on their toes.

The final stage of learning occurs when the diver reaches the "unconscious-competent" level. This is akin to someone who has been driving a car for a long time. They make their daily commute and barely recall the route they took or the things they saw along the way. When this occurs in cave diving, it is often the point when complacency kicks in.

I have often felt that cave divers with roughly 50-100 hours after initial training, may be at the greatest risk, especially if nothing has scared them along the way. A serious gear malfunction in that timeframe often frightens the diver back to the previous level of learning, when they become conscious, diligent divers again. A long absence from diving will also result in the diver stepping backwards in the model until they catch up with their skills and practice.

To avoid the pitfalls of complacency, good procedures and a commitment to pre-dive checks are critical. A diver who carefully reviews their personal preparedness as well as their equipment readiness will be better prepared to deal with the issues on the road ahead.

Communication

Divers use a variety of techniques to communicate underwater. Hand signals, light signals, slates and notebooks are effective, while CCR cave divers find that speaking clearly can often be heard by other divers who are also using rebreathers.

Hand Signals

There are three command signals in cave diving that include: call the dive, hold, and okay. Each of these three signals is answered with the same signal if understood or affirmative. There are numerous other signals in common use including the ones pictured here. When using hand signals, the diver should carefully illuminate the hand making the signal with regard to the other diver's point of view. Try not to blind the other divers in the process of communication. Ensure that your buddies are fluent in the same hand signals that you are so there are no misunderstandings underwater.

The okay sign is a command signal, which is answered in the affirmative with the same signal. "Hold" and "Call the dive" are the other two command signals, which are answered with a mirrored response when understood. Photo by Jill Heinerth

Hand Signals for Cave Divers

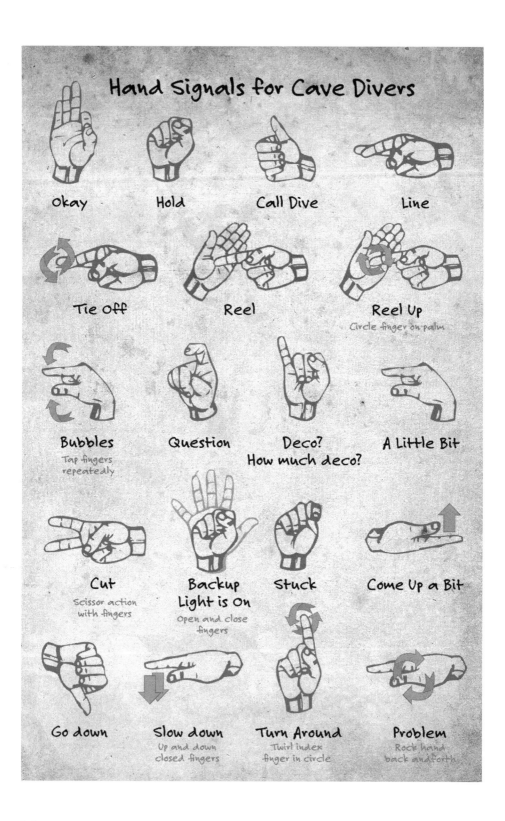

Okay

Hold

Call Dive

Line

Tie Off

Reel

Reel Up
Circle finger on palm

Bubbles
Tap fingers repeatealy

Question

Deco?
How much deco?

A Little Bit

Cut
Scissor action with fingers

Backup
Light is On
Open and close fingers

Stuck

Come Up a Bit

Go down

Slow down
Up and down closed fingers

Turn Around
Twirl index finger in circle

Problem
Rock hand back andforth

Number Signals

One   Two   Three   Four   Five

Six   Seven   Eight

Nine   Zero   Ten

Signals done in sequence

Light Signals

Light signals are the most actively used communication technique in caves. Generally, the team leader initiates an okay signal, and the second diver responds by slowly circling their light over the beam of the team leader. The third diver in the team replies by circling his/her light over the beam of the second diver in succession. The motion is slow and controlled so it is not mistaken for a more urgent call to action.

If you need to gain the attention of a diver in the team, slowly sweep your light beam across another team member's beam. This back and forth motion alerts them to respond to your problem.

Very fast back and forth motions of a light indicates an emergency situation and should be immediately answered by moving towards the diver to assist.

Slates and Notebooks

Wrist slates are convenient for complex written communications or backup dive tables. Notebooks may be similarly used and stored in a hip pocket when not in use. Dangling slates are not suitable for streamlining in caves.

Audio Communications

Rebreather divers may attempt verbal communication through clear enunciation of words, but if you require clean audio for a specific purpose, full-face masks (FFMs) may be employed. FFMs are not common in cave diving. They can create a carbon dioxide build-up risk, and limit a diver's mobility and peripheral vision. Furthermore, FFMs are extremely difficult to clear after flooding and may need to be ditched in an air supply emergency. Generally, scientists, commercial divers and filmmakers only use these as a tool.

Propulsion and Trim

Fin Kicking Techniques

Fin techniques vary greatly from kicking styles that are used in open water. With limited space and greater opportunities for silting, cave divers must be extremely aware of the path of destruction they may be leaving behind. There is almost no cave where full flutter kicking can be tolerated without silting problems. Most divers try to use a frog-style kick to achieve maximum propulsion while avoiding forces directed towards the floor of the cave.

A modified flutter kick may sometimes be suitable. In this case, the diver bends their knees to raise their feet up off the floor of the cave and kicks from the ankle instead of the hip with very small up and down flexing of the fin.

Sculling and modified frog kicks shrink a frog motion to an ankle-only kick that brings the foot soles towards each other with sideways force.

Pull and Pull

In some cases, the flow of water will overpower the diver and leave them unable to make headway using only fins. In this case, it is acceptable to contact the cave with your hands to pull yourself along. This technique has been referred to as "pull and glide," however, if you are able to glide after pulling, it is doubtful whether you ever needed to pull through the cave at all. If you must "pull and pull" to make forward progress then, cave contact is warranted.

If you choose to pull yourself through the cave, try to stay on the trail of contact that has been made by other divers. Use a small portion of your hand or a single finger to place on a rock outcropping, then gingerly pull your body beyond your hand placement without dragging your skin across the surface of the rock. Many new cave divers injure their fingers during their cave class when they unnecessarily drag their flesh across hard surfaces. After practice, this tendency can be completely avoided and "cave fingers" will be avoided.

Some sites, such as Cow Springs, in Florida, contain a heavy rope, which runs alongside the cave guideline. This heavy guideline is intended for pulling so that delicate rock formations can remain pristine. Never use a regular guideline for pulling through a cave as it may become damaged or broken.

Cave fingers might be a "badge of courage" when you are early in your training, but an experienced cave diver learns how to avoid this. Photo: Jill Heinerth

Touch Contact

When visibility declines to zero, a team is forced to navigate out of the cave environment by feel. Each team member should immediately find the line and place a loose, but secure, okay signal on the line, overlapping fingers so the line is not kicked away by another diver. Once oriented to the exit direction, the lead diver should wait for contact from the remaining team members. On the line and in touch contact, divers use a series of hand signals to exit the cave as a team. The team travels in single file on the guideline, while keeping contact with the line and each other. Placing your hand on the shin of the diver in front of you will allow them to continue to use their fins effectively without kicking you in the head.

When a diver pushes forward, that indicates "go." Pulling back, means "reverse." This is used to tell the team to back up, perhaps to deal with an entanglement. A squeeze indicates "stop," and several successive, urgent squeezes, signals an emergency situation such as "need air." If a diver loses contact with you, that also indicates stop. They may have lost the line or they may be dealing with issues requiring two hands. Once they re-establish contact and give a push signal, the team continues their exit.

Experienced teams develop a looser form of contact known as "touch and go." In this formula, the trailing diver continually reaches forward and pushes the diver in front to move along. If contact is lost for a period, the lead diver pauses until the next touch and go, or backs up slowly until contact is re-established.

Guideline

Failure to run a continuous guideline to the surface is one of leading causes of fatalities in cave diving. Therefore it is important to become proficient and comfortable at running reels. Guidelines are used as a visual reference most of the time, but when visibility is reduced, a diver can follow the line by touch.

Tie Offs and Placements

A primary tie-off should be made in the open water environment, sometimes right at the surface when visibility conditions are poor. Care should be taken to ensure this tie-off cannot be untied in the diver's absence. A secondary tie-off is made just inside the overhead environment. Since this serves as a backup to the primary tie-off, care should be taken to ensure it is secure and does not damage the cave. After the two initial tie-offs, placements are pre-

ferred over additional tie-offs. Placements route the line around a protruding rock or object rather than wrapping the line around an outcropping. Wraps are more difficult to follow when visibility is lost, and when they break away; they cause slack line that can drift into line traps or cause entanglements.

A guideline in Greater Exuma is coated with marine life. The two arrows point towards separate entrances, but a diver should always return the way they came from. You can never be certain that a line is intact or that you will be able to find the exit from the end of a line that has not been connected to open water. Photo: Jill Heinerth

Where possible, the line should be laid close to the floor and off to the side, so that a diver may swim beside or above the line while visually referencing its location. The line should be laid in such a way that divers may easily follow the course using touch contact if they have to exit without visibility. In caves where the rock is soft, silt screws or pegs can be used as placements or tie-off points. Silt screws can be made of short lengths of PVC pipe that are notched to hold a line in place. These devices can be cut at a 45-degree angle to make them easier to push into the soft floor when tie-offs and placements are not available. Metal silt screws and extra long tent pegs are commercially available.

Laying and Retrieving Line

When running a line, a diver should hold the reel well away from their body to prevent entanglement hazards. A finger can be used as a brake on the reel barrel to prevent the line from running away too quickly and jamming in the body of the reel. Maintaining tension on the line, the diver makes their tie-offs and placements, which are checked by the second team member for security.

When the guideline is reeled up, the team leader (the reel runner) first ensures that the entire team is on the exit side of the reel. The team leader picks up the reel and slowly winds up the guideline, carefully weaving it back and forth so it does not spill over the sides of the barrel. Maintaining tension is the key for preventing reel jams. If slack line is encountered, the diver ahead of the reel picks up the slack and helps to maintain a taut lie for the reel man. The slack line is slowly fed back as the reel man catches up.

Two divers work together to create a secure secondary tie-off. Photo: Jill Heinerth

Rules of the Road

Guidelines that are laid from the open water to the main line are called temporary lines. These lines are generally only left in place for the duration of a dive, but are sometimes left in place for longer periods when a team is setting up a complex dive plan. These lines should never be removed in an effort to "clean up" since they could be vital safety gear set in place for a team that is coming from another entry point. Each diver in a team should place a personal marker on their primary reel line where it connects to the main permanent guideline. This acts as a simple accounting procedure.

When high diver traffic creates an entrance hazard, teams can arrange to share one reel to the permanent guideline. Prior to diving, two teams can agree to share a reel, and every diver agrees to place a unique marker on the line on the exit side of the reel. When a team reaches the reel on their exit, each diver removes their unique marker. If the second team finds only their markers in place, they can safely remove the reel, comfortable that the other team has left the cave. No one should attempt to share a reel unless arrangements have been made before entering the water.

If multiple lines are present, divers should try to avoid sharing tie-offs and placements. Line should always be laid underneath another team's line with the assumption that the team already inside will be exiting first. Care should be taken to run the line without crossing the tunnel or crossing over other lines so that each team can easily retrieve theirs in reverse order of entry.

Permanent guidelines are laid in many caves around the world to keep divers on well-traveled routes. In locations where delicate ceiling decorations might be harmed by percolation, these guidelines also keep divers on a path that preserves the rest of a large room, understanding that even bubbles hitting he ceiling can alter or damage formations. Permanent guidelines are often made of heavy, yellow Kernmantle line, offering abrasion resistance and high visibility.

Line tension is critical every step of the dive. Line should never be allowed to fall loose around a placement. It should be carefully tensioned and belayed or anchored with a twist and overlap that increases tension as you pull the real forward. The anchor point indicates the side of placement the diver should swim on. In the case above, the anchor tells the diver to stay on the side of sign with the words "no parking." Close adherence to details such as this will prevent a slow exit if visibility is lost. Photos: Jill Heinerth

The Primary tie-off is placed in the open water and a secondary tie-off is made just inside the cavern zone. In general, placements are preferred after those initial secure tie-offs. Photo: Jill Heinerth

Crossing a Gap

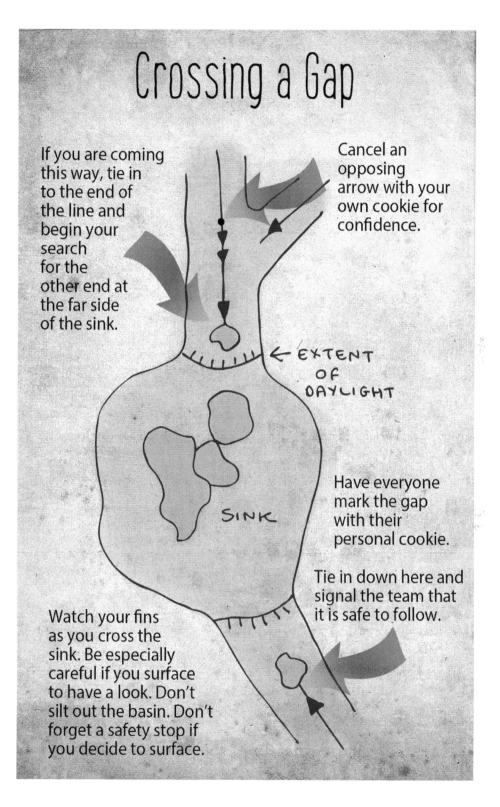

If you are coming this way, tie in to the end of the line and begin your search for the other end at the far side of the sink.

Cancel an opposing arrow with your own cookie for confidence.

← EXTENT OF DAYLIGHT

SINK

Have everyone mark the gap with their personal cookie.

Tie in down here and signal the team that it is safe to follow.

Watch your fins as you cross the sink. Be especially careful if you surface to have a look. Don't silt out the basin. Don't forget a safety stop if you decide to surface.

Popular routes are laid with a single continuous guideline. In caverns, in locations such as Mexico, popular routes encircle the daylight zone of a large cavern. The permanent guideline into the cave passage is placed as a separate line that is generally not attached to this route. When many branching conduits offer several popular routes, these side passages are separated from the main line, and the space between lines is "jumped" with a temporary jump/gap reel. Technically speaking, a jump is a space that is filled with a reel, creating a "T' in the line. A gap bridges the empty space between the ends of two lines. However, within the community, you will find these terms are often used almost interchangeably.

In some parts of the world, especially in colder environments and exploratory caves, divers will encounter a greater number of "Ts" in the line. These Ts can create confusion, and should be marked with directional arrows or other markers that aid in navigation. Your marker should always point out of the cave.

Exploratory tunnels are often lined with lighter gauge string. Divers trying to pack a lot of line onto an exploration reel use lighter, less expensive line. This line is usually knotted every ten feet in North America or every three or five meters in other parts of the world. The knots create distance reference for the diver's survey. These lines are more fragile than permanent Kernmantle guideline and care should be taken to inspect exploration line if you follow it into a new passage. Divers can expect heavy percolation in these tunnels since the passage is not as well traveled.

When the lead diver ties into the permanent guideline, they should mark their reel line with personal marker such as a cookie or REM. Each other member of the team can quickly drop a marker on the same line. When the team returns to their reel, they can easily recognize their gear, remove their personal marker and take out the reel.

Marking the Line

Divers use triangular line arrows, also known as "dorf" markers or line markers, to indicate the direction to the nearest exit point. Permanent line arrows can be found in popular caves every one- to five-hundred feet. These permanent markers are often inscribed with the distance to the nearest opening. In Europe, lines are sometimes marked with zip ties or duct tape. Do not remove or disturb permanent markers.

Two line arrows placed closely together and pointing in the same direction, designates a location where divers can jump to a popular side passage. The side passage is usually perpendicular to the arrows and very close by, generally within easy sight. Line arrows placed back-to-back on the guideline mark the halfway point between two "end of line" locations. There may be openings nearby but an additional reel may be needed to surface from an "end of line." In some locations such as Mexico, double line arrows inscribed with the word AIR direct the diver to a safe breathable air bell in the ceiling.

Divers should always plan to return to the entrance from which they entered, unless a more complex dive has been previously arranged and safely setup. A line arrow pointing towards a secondary opening, further into the cave, may not connect to open water. Furthermore, one cannot assume that the guideline is intact or that the passage is clear.

Divers should carry an assortment of personalized line markers that they can use as navigational aids during their dive. For penetration/distance markers on complex dive plans, divers use non-directional line markers called cookies or REMs. Some divers use clothespins as non-directional line markers. Line arrows and cookies should be locked onto the line with a double loop (if possible) to ensure that they stay in place and cannot be easily dislodged by a misplaced fin kick.

Double locked line arrows pointing the same direction on a permanent line may indicate the location of a popular jump. Drawing: Jill Heinerth

Making Jumps

When making a jump from the main line to a side passage, the diver deploys a jump reel or spool. The line is looped around the main guideline and marked

103

with a line arrow if none are present. If permanent double arrows are present, they can be used for this purpose. Each team member leaves a personal cookie at this location marking the way out of the cave. The reel is run over to the new guideline and looped once around the line and clipped off on itself and secured with a twist. A few popular jumps have a permanent device called a "snap and gap." In this case, a piece of line or bungee is attached permanently to the end of the side passage line. When a diver wishes to travel in that tunnel, they simply reach over and bridge the gap by snapping the clip onto the main line in between double line arrows. They also place their own personal marker indicating the exit direction. These devices have lost their popularity over the years because multiple teams traveling in the same tunnel can get confused over whether this should be unsnapped or left attached upon departure. One such device can be found on the jump from the main line in Madison Blue cave in Florida, to the Martz Sink line.

Each diver leaves a personal marker on the jump as an attendance marker and indication of a navigational choice. Photo: Jill Heinerth

Crossing Ts

A "T" or "Y" junction in a cave indicates a navigational choice. If you encounter a location where the line branches in two or more directions, then each team member should mark the exit side of the junction with a personal marker. This ensures that you will know which way to go when you return to the junction and want to exit the cave. These markers also serve as attendance markers, letting team members know where to search when they have lost their buddy. These markers also let other divers know how many people are in a passage, which may not comfortably support a large number of divers. If you see a lot of markers on a jump, you may want to go to another part of the cave to avoid delays and diver congestion.

Unfortunately many divers violate basic safety rules by making visual jumps and not using markers. But, the dive is not about the destination, it is also about completing a beautifully engineered safe dive that you can be proud of.

Making a Jump

Many major jumps are marked with permanent double line arrows.

Place your line in between those arrows or use your own arrow.
Check for local preferences.

Each diver uses a personal marker on exit side of arrows.

Allow the team leader time to find the line in the side passage. Stay on the main line until the lead diver signals that he/she has secured the line. Check it as you swim over to see if it will be in the way of other teams and fix, as necessary.

Canceling Markers

There are times when you might be "swimming against the grain." In other words, you are swimming into the cave but encountering arrows that point to another exit. At each of these navigation points, the team leader should illuminate the marker and seek a confirmation light signal that other team members are aware of the contrary arrow. You can "cancel" an arrow, by placing your own cookie on the exit side of the arrow. This indicates to your team, the direction in which you intend to exit the cave. Canceling arrows may add to your confidence and also offer a tactile reference in the event of a light or visibility failure.

The double back-to-back arrows represent the halfway point between two ends of line. The personal marker is a confidence indicator reminding the diver which of these directions is relevant to their successful exit. After placing a marker like this one, you should signal the rest of the team for confirmation. Photo: Jill Heinerth

Complex Navigation

When a complex dive plan calls for a team to enter one site and exit from another, the team must plan a series of dives in order to conduct the traverse safely. The first dive is conducted in the upstream direction. The team travels until a member reaches their turn pressure. The line is marked with a non-directional line marker such as a cookie and the team retreats, leaving any reels in place. The second dive is conducted in the downstream direction from another opening. Bearing in mind extra conservatism for a downstream dive, the team attempts to reach their line marker before their turnaround pressure.

If they reach the marker, then the entire team can complete the through-trip with the satisfaction that they have adequate gas supplies. They remove reels once they know they are safely outbound. A third short dive is often needed to retrieve the reel in the downstream entrance. This dive is referred to as a cleanup dive.

106

Planning a Traverse

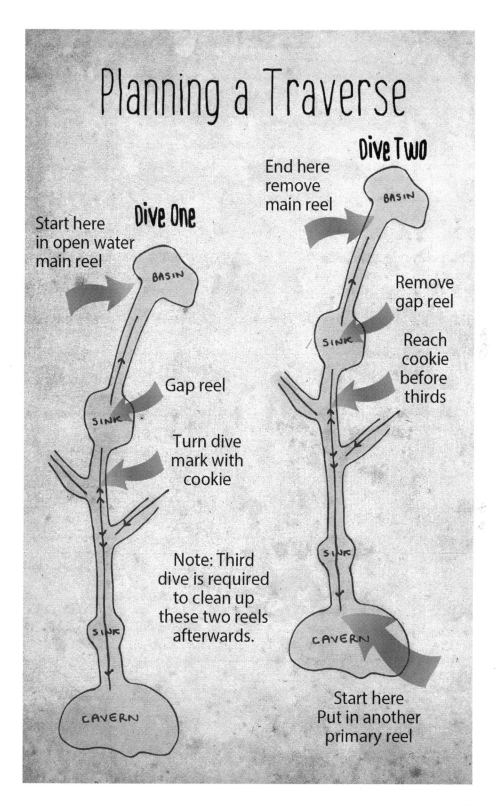

Dive One

Start here
in open water
main reel

BASIN

Gap reel

SINK

Turn dive
mark with
cookie

Note: Third
dive is required
to clean up
these two reels
afterwards.

SINK

CAVERN

Dive Two

End here
remove
main reel

BASIN

Remove
gap reel

SINK

Reach
cookie
before
thirds

SINK

CAVERN

Start here
Put in another
primary reel

Circular routes are planned in much the same way. A circuit dive has the same entry and exit point, but takes the divers on a circular route. The same procedures are used as a traverse with a set-up dive followed by a circuit dive where the reels are removed.

Due to their complex nature, circuits and traverses are not introduced until a cave diver nears completion of their Full Cave/Cave Two training program. These dives require planning and patience, and divers should never attempt circuits and traverses without installing appropriate reels where gaps and jumps exist. Just because you completed a particular traverse on another occasion does not mean the passage will be clear or the line intact on another occasion. This author has reminded divers that, "geologic time includes now." In the past twenty years, several caves have been changed dramatically after seasonal floods. Hart Springs has had entrances change and collapse while others opened. A rock fell in Challenge Sink at Peacock Springs, sealing that exit until divers could launch a campaign to remove the obstruction. Although there is only one instance of a cave diver being buried during an underwater landslide, divers would be best to remember that caves are always evolving. Well-organized dive plans and strict adherence to safety protocols should prevent most incidents.

During cave training you will learn how to setup and attempt a circuit. Successful completion of this drill might include turning the dive before you are able to make the circular route. No prudent instructor will punish you for aborting early. On the other hand, if you stretch gas supplies beyond a safe turn pressure in order to compete a task, then a good instructor will hold you back until you can display safer diving practices. Photo: Jill Heinerth

Planning a Circuit

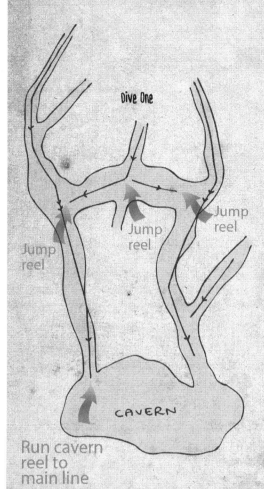

Dive One

Jump reel

Jump reel

Jump reel

CAVERN

Run cavern reel to main line

Plan on running one primary reel and three jumps (mark each appropriatly with personal markers), then mark the max penetration with a cookie, based on available gas supply. Retreat and leave all the reels and markers in place.

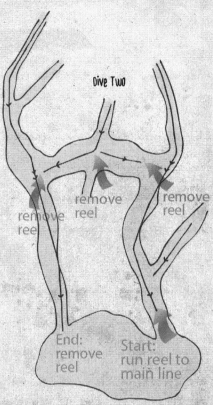

Dive Two

remove reel

remove reel

remove reel

End: remove reel

Start: run reel to main line

Start on the right side of cavern. Put in a primary reel to permanent guideline. Reach cookie before turn pressure. Remove the rest of reels on exit.

Contingency: If we don't make the dive as planned there is always a continuous guideline to the exit.

When a diver chooses to swim across a gap or a jump without laying a guideline, this is referred to as a visual gap or visual jump. Visual gaps leave the diver without a continuous guideline to the surface – one of the leading causes of fatalities within cave systems.

A guideline is a lifeline, offering divers their only direct connection to the surface and safety. As such, guidelines should be treated with care. They are intended as visual reference, but divers should also reference the geology and structure of their surroundings. The guideline can be used as a tactile reference when exiting under reduced visibility, but never pull on the line since fragile tie-offs can break or the line itself can be compromised. Divers should patch any frayed or damaged line they encounter, and loose, abandoned guidelines should be removed from the cave.

Guideline Emergencies

Line Traps

If the line is poorly laid through a passage, it may fall into a place where a diver cannot physically pass. This is called a line trap. Line traps may occur when the line is placed carelessly and allowed to fall out of its intended location. They may also occur when tie-offs or placements come undone or the rock to which they are tied, breaks. Caves with friable rock are difficult places to lay line effectively and extra time should be budgeted during the planning of these dives.

Entanglement

When a diver becomes entangled in a permanent line or their own reel, they should make one attempt to free themselves and then signal for assistance. If a diver becomes hopelessly entangled and the guideline must be severed, then extra precautions need to be taken to ensure the safety of the team. First, the entire team must be put on the exit side of the entanglement. Then the guideline is cut and repaired if time allows. If a repair cannot be made, then loose ends of the line should be tied off or secured somehow. Other teams in the area can be alerted to make the appropriate repairs.

Broken Line

When a broken line is encountered, it should be repaired with line from your safety reel. If your team comes across a broken line when exiting the cave, you should secure and tie to the end of the guideline and carefully assess your surroundings. You should look for familiar territory, bubbles on the ceiling and obvious signs of diver traffic such as silt hanging in the water column, rocks rubbed clean from traffic and line furrows in the bottom. Using flow as another indication of exit direction, you should carefully strike out in the obvious direction while unspooling line while continually assessing your surroundings. Once the guideline has been found, you should make the repair and exit the cave. Lost divers must consciously avoid the temptation to swim into clear water, since the way you traveled before will invariably be filled with more silt than a tunnel not previously traveled. It is prudent for divers to rehearse knot-tying drills on land and underwater so that reliable repairs can be made underwater when needed.

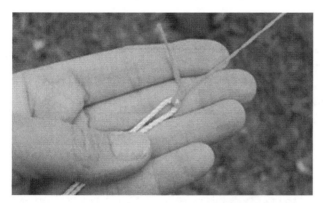

Your instructor will show you how to cleanly repair a broken guideline and how to escape a hopeless entanglement with a proper line repair. Compromised or broken guidelines should always be reported to the local safety committee who can ensure the popular line is checked and repaired if necessary. Photo: Jill Heinerth

Lost Line

If you lose the guideline, you should immediately stop and assess your environment. Look for silt, ceiling bubbles and the lights of the remaining dive team. After shielding your light against your chest, slowly sweep the beam around the cave corridor in the hopes of signaling teammates. The next step is to make a secure tie off with a safety reel and travel in the direction that seems obvious. If visibility has been lost, then you should begin to search low to the floor and continue until you

If you need to momentarily secure a spool in the course of a search or line repair, secure the line, reel and the clip. Photo: Jill Heinerth

reach a wall, while sweeping widely with an outstretched arm to find the guideline. Traveling up the wall, continue to unspool line until you detect that you are creating slack. Complete a circular sweep, slowly reeling in your line and hopefully snagging the main guideline in the process. Once back at the secure tie off, you can search in a different direction and continue your search until the guideline has been found.

Once you have recovered the main line, tie off your safety reel as you would a jump and place an arrow in the direction of your travel or fasten the clip pointing in the direction you intend to swim. Then work your way toward the exit. If you do not find your team upon exiting, review your gas supply and decide if re-entering the cave makes sense. Hopefully, your teammates will find your safety reel and personalized arrow or clip and know that you are moving toward the exit.

Rosemary Lunn practices her lost line drill during cave diver training. During this drill trainees wear a mask blackout cover to simulate loss of visibility. Photo: Jill Heinerth

Lost Buddy

When the team realizes that they have lost a diver, they should immediately assess their surroundings, taking careful stock of ceiling bubbles, silt, side passages and other environmental clues. Place a directional arrow at your current location, pointing the way to the exit. The team then retreats to the last known location of their colleague and looks for obvious signs of a diver's passage. The team shields their lights and searches for the light of the lost diver, gently sweeping a light towards any probable location. If the team finds a side passage that seems like an obvious search point, one member secures a reel onto the main guideline and marks it with an arrow pointing toward the exit. Generally, one diver reels down the side passage while the remaining team members stay in place with their bodies oriented towards the exit. Once the diver has been located, they are placed on the exit side of the reel and brought back to the marked guideline. The arrow on the main line alleviates any confusion and the body language of the remaining team members clearly demonstrates the way to the exit.

In many cases, a lost diver does not realize they are lost. It is not uncommon for divers to make an accidental jump by swimming into another passage with line. This can happen in caves with very good visibility when divers tend to stray farther off the guideline as they navigate through the environment. Photo: Jill Heinerth

In no case should searchers risk their own lives to locate a lost teammate. The "lost" diver may have already exited the cave safely. Remaining gas can be recalculated and stretched based on current situational awareness, but no one should search beyond the ability to make a safe exit from the cave. Consider how far it is to the exit and how much gas will be needed to get you there. Decide whether you want to retain enough for an out of air partner or will take the risk that they are lost and not also low on gas. Determine if you are psychologically prepared to take on the additional risk. Think about whether exiting and getting help might be the most effective course of action. Nobody can make these difficult choices for you. It should be part of an honest risk assessment and action plan made well before any dive.

If you reach their point where you are no longer comfortable searching, place a line arrow pointing out of the cave and clip a backup light to the guideline and turn it on. This signal will indicate to the lost buddy that you have abandoned the search and have exited. In the event that they need a light, you have left them with a critical piece of safety gear. Review this procedure with new teammates before diving so everyone understands the signal. In the event that other teams are dispatched in a search, your initial arrow and light/arrow combination will help define the area that has been searched.

Before attempting any underwater line drills, your instructor will conduct topside training that will help you master the necessary skills and prepare your equipment properly. Photo: Jill Heinerth

Topside Practice Drills

Practice or review the following procedures before you even get wet:

- Running and retrieving guidelines

- Primary and secondary tie offs, placement and line traps

- Roles of dive team/positioning/teamwork/right of way

- Following the line in a silt out using touch contact procedures

- Procedures for using line markers: At permanent guideline, in the event of buddy/team separation, cancelling, etc.

- Lost line procedure including tie in to permanent guideline with and without visibility

- Lost diver procedure including procedures for abandoning a search and team roles and responsibilities when putting in a T

- Entanglement procedure and patching a broken guideline

- Air sharing team protocols with and without visibility

- Light failure positioning

- Valve shutdowns for twinset or sidemount

- Hand signals

- S-Drill procedures

114

**DIVE
PLANNING**

CHAPTER

Dive Planning ---

Pre-Dive Prep

To safely dive in caves, your gear must be in top condition. Even a small leak should not be tolerated when diving in the overhead environment. Test your equipment before a trip to ensure that you catch any problems before you get to the water, and keep your gear on a regular maintenance cycle. Place a reminder alarm in your smart phone calendar to remind you about appropriate service intervals for your gear.

One of the best sources of specific site information is the Internet. Site maps, condition reports, access policies and even videos are all found online. Some divers seek out videos that show them how to find the main line and how to get into the water. Cave diving groups and forums provide an opportunity to find buddies, vet operators and guides, find information on access procedures and learn about current site status.

Personal Preparation

Personal preparation includes physical training, practice, fitness, hydration, diet and psychological readiness. Stating the obvious, you should be current in your skills; healthy and psychologically prepared for the environment you have chosen. There are days when any one of these factors could be compromised, and those are the days to consider hanging up your fins. Each decision you make about your readiness to dive becomes a decision for the entire team. Any additional risks you assume will be risks they face as well.

In selecting a team, you should find common objectives and a similar philosophy in diving. An ideal cave diving team is considered to be three people. With three people, redundancy of gear is enhanced and air-sharing options are improved. A team of two is acceptable, but four people should be divided into two separate teams, rather than trying to dive together as a large group.

Planning Objectives

Plans should be made to accommodate the comfort and background of the least experienced diver. In many ways, the lion's share of work happens before you hit the water. Planning a smooth operation augments enjoyment as well as safety. When you begin to formulate a plan, consider the following:

- Experience/training level of team members
- Physical requirements of site

116

- Dive equipment (What will be needed and is it maintained and ready?)

- Contingency equipment (Who will bring spare parts?)

- Emergency equipment (Who is responsible for providing emergency equipment?)

- Logistical requirements of site access [certification cards, fee (often cash only in small bills), special permits, wheeled dolly for gear, etc.]

- Topside comfort (thermal, hydration, food, chairs, etc.)

- Preparation area (Where do you assemble gear? Do you need a table, tarp, tailgate, rain cover?)

- Distance to entry point (walking, hand carts, packs, spelunking, boats, other access)

- Entry (How and where do you enter water safely to preserve visibility?)

- Dive objectives

- Risk assessment and assumption or mitigation of risks (Are the stairs slippery, can you scrub them to make them safer to climb? Is the entry ladder safe or should you replace it or plan an alternate exit technique if it breaks?)

- Team leadership assignments

- Planned depth (appropriate gas END, O_2, etc.)

- Planned time (turn pressures, stamina, thermal, decompression, equipment limitations such as light burn time, rebreather consumables, psychological readiness)

- Contingency plan (How do you survive unplanned extensions in depth and time?)

- Emergency plan (EMS, evacuation plan, personal information regarding team members, location of keys to vehicles, cell phones, readiness and location of emergency equipment and assurance everyone can operate it, DAN insurance information, emergency contact details)

Risk Assessment

With the tools needed to complete record-breaking dives only a credit card swipe away, technical divers all over the world are experiencing a paradigm shift. There are fewer novices dying in underwater caves. Three decades ago, there were a great number of open water instructors with decent diving experience meeting their end in caves, unaware of the basic safety techniques required of cave divers. However, there is an upward trend of accidents involving experienced cave divers who choose to exceed their training and experience.

Instructors create a partnership with their students by helping them to master specific diving skills. When cave divers act as role models, they discuss their mistakes and share personal motivations for diving. Ultimately, we can all play a part in a diver's quest for knowledge, but only real-world diving experience will permanently shape behavior beyond our watchful eyes. Instructors can't dictate choice. They can only hope that their students carefully consider each risk before every dive.

Too Safe for Comfort

In the 1970s, automakers concluded that anti-lock brakes would reduce the rate of skids and rollovers. With a well-earned reputation for innovative safety features, Volvo automobiles enjoyed increased sales. Soccer moms loaded their kids in the back, with the illusion that the new technology would increase their safety envelope. Unfortunately, research has proven that although people perceived their risk as reduced, they actually drove more aggressively and had just as many accidents.

Like automobile drivers, when divers perceive conditions as less risky, they tend to take on more risk. When conditions are unknown and the perils seem great, people tend to act more conservatively.

Running Scared

Modern diving equipment, such as closed-circuit rebreathers and Class-A scuba regulators, has reduced the frequency of gear failures. Many CCR divers log hundreds of incident-free dives. However, most experienced rebreather divers can recount an incident when they realized that complacency had crept into their performance and left them vulnerable to having an incident or accident. The lucky ones learn from those experiences. The unlucky ones either quit or die. A certain amount of fear equates to a healthy respect for life.

The Alpine Approach

As the reliability of equipment increases our range and capability in diving, the lure of the "hero-dive" is hard to ignore. We can go deeper, stay longer and explore places never seen by man. Rumors spread on Internet forums and dive blogs about virgin cave passages, seducing divers to leave their mark in technical diving history. When planned carefully, exploration opportunities can be rewarding. But ill-conceived, or intensely goal-oriented dives often lead to disaster.

118

Technical divers are often compared to mountain climbers. But, the mountain climber that runs up Everest without a tent, pack or supplemental oxygen, puts more people than himself at risk. If he is lucky, he will make a speed record and gain a notch for his summit-belt. If he retreats in a storm, desperation may lead to stealing staged food, tents and oxygen tanks from another team. In the worst-case scenario, some well-meaning rescuer may lose their life in attempts to return his body to base camp.

Climbers on the world's greatest summits now walk past the remains of less fortunate climbers. They stop for a moment of reflection with "Green-Boots" or "the guy from the storm of 1998." If you think the technical diving community has not already reached that phase in its development, think again. Wreck warriors in the northeast U.S. have conveniently left body recoveries for the end of a big dive weekend - and at least seven caves have become permanent tombs for cave divers.

Personal Preparation

As more fixed ropes and guide operations escort unprepared tourists up the face of Everest, we are reminded of the simple fact that when Mother Nature displays her ferocity, each climber or diver is reduced to their own capabilities and equipment.

When I certify a student at any level of diving, I ask myself if that person is capable of self-rescue and capable of buddy-rescue in conditions similar to or perhaps worse those of their certification level. I can sign them off on their behavior and performance at a given level, but must rely on them to continue to make good choices in the future.

Motivations

Whether it is the environment, camaraderie or technology, most people commence their diving career for good reason - for a love of the sport.

Age and experience should be accompanied by wisdom, and a renewed understanding that we are not invincible. My very capable and experienced colleagues and I turn down more expeditions than we accept. The risk is sometimes not worth the rewards of the undertaking.

As you develop your skills and increase the size of your gear locker, remember to stay realistic in your objectives. Be patient and careful as you choose to incrementally increase risk and be content with your participation at any level. If you achieve your goal of reaching the mountain summit, or the end of the line in the cave, then that is icing on the cake. But no matter the investment in

119

time and money, be prepared to walk away a few feet short of the goal. Ultimately, the only successful expeditions are the ones from which you and the entire team return safely.

The Steps

Risk assumption varies for every individual and will change throughout your lifetime. Ultimately, you will need to find divers that fit with your desired risk profile and should stay away from others that increase your personal risk. Dives should always be planned for the least capable team member, yet everyone on the team must carry with them, the ability and willingness for self- and buddy-rescue.

Risk assumption includes a frank discussion with your family members so that they have an understanding about your personal motivations for technical diving. They deserve the respect of having a say in your activities. If you are the family breadwinner or have dependents that rely on you, it would be selfish to ignore them in your assumption of risk. Many cave divers have set aside their fins while their children are in their formative years, only returning to the sport after the child has reached maturity and self-sufficiency. It behooves you to consider the worst-case scenario and whether those risks can be mitigated or accepted by the entire family unit.

Risk assessment also requires a frank review of your personal health and fitness. If you are unwell, unfit or under a physician's care, is it really fair to put your buddy at risk too? Every decision you make will be one that your team may have to live or die for. If you dive with your spouse, what expectations are assumed? In the case of separation will you search until the bitter end, leaving the kids without parents? Will you save yourself? Will you carry the survivor's guilt until it eats away at your soul? Do you have life insurance? A will? Advanced medical directives? Somebody in your family that knows what to do? These are difficult topics indeed, but ones that should be discussed and considered every time you go diving. Although my husband is not a cave diver, I take him with me spiritually every time I enter the water and make the best decisions for both of us at all times. If you can't face these serious discussions, perhaps you should reconsider engaging in what the world deems to be the most dangerous sport.

Dive Logistics

Gas Planning and Fills

One of the first things to figure out when you are planning a dive is how much gas you consume on an ideal dive. Technical divers calculate a figure known as Surface Air Consumption Rate (SAC) to help them compare air consumption with other team members. To calculate this figure, divers can swim for 10-minutes at a given, stable depth and correlate that air consumption to an equivalent surface figure in the following way:

Calculating your SAC Rate

IMPERIAL EXAMPLE

a. In ten minutes I used _____ psi from my double tanks at depth.

b. Therefore in one minute I used _____ psi from my double tanks at depth.

[a / 10]

c. The average depth during the swim was _____ feet.

d. The average pressure during the swim was _____ ATA. [depth / 33) + 1]

e. The amount of air I used in my tanks in one minute at the surface is _____ psi.

[b / d]

f. In a single tank I would have used _____ psi in one minute at the surface.

[e x 2]

g. My tanks are _____ cu ft. rated at _____ psi working pressure.*

*You can find these embossed numbers on the crown of your tank.

h. Every time I breathe _____ psi, I will use one cubic foot from my tanks.

[working pressure / capacity in cu ft.]

i. Since I used _____ psi per minute, my SAC rate is _____ cu ft. / min.

[f / h]

METRIC EXAMPLE

a. In ten minutes I used _____ bar from my double tanks at depth.

b. Therefore in one minute I used _____ bar from my double tanks at depth.

[a / 10]

c. The average depth during the swim was _____ meters.

d. The average pressure during the swim was _____ ATA. [depth / 10) + 1]

e. The amount of gas I used in my tanks in one minute at the surface is _____ bar. [b / d]

f. In a single tank I would have used _____ bar in one minute at the surface. This is my SAC rate. [e x 2]

Calculated in this manner, the SAC rate is an ideal figure that must be padded for less than ideal scenarios. Some divers calculate their SAC rate under high workload so they have a range of numbers that can be used in dive planning.

Tank Baseline

When tanks are filled, they rarely get filled precisely to their working pressure. If using the imperial measurement system, we need to compare gas volumes between different members of the dive team. After the tank has been filled, we can use a number called a "tank baseline" to compare volumes between different fills and different sizes of tanks. The baseline tells us how many cu. ft. are represented by one psi on the diver's gauge.

Tank Baseline = Cubic Foot Capacity x 2 Tanks / Tank Working Pressure

If Diver A uses double LP 104s, they would calculate:

Baseline = 104 x 2 / 2640 = .078 cu. ft. per psi

If Diver B used double aluminum 80s, they would calculate:

80 x 2 / 3000 = .053 cu. ft. per psi

To calculate the total volume in a diver's doubles, simply multiply the tank baseline by the actual fill pressure.

For example: if Diver A has 104 cu. ft. steel tanks with 2500 psi, they would calculate:

.078 x 2500 = 195 cu. ft. of gas

If Diver B has 80 aluminum tanks with 2500 psi in the tanks.

.053 x 2500 = 132.5 cu. ft. of gas

If these divers simply compared their gas supply using their pressure gauges, they could get into trouble. If the diver using large tanks had a failure, the diver with the aluminum 80s needs to ensure that she has reserved adequate gas to get both divers safely to the surface.

Rule of Thirds

The "rule of thirds" is used by cave divers to calculate a safe turn pressure for the dive. The turn pressure is a minimum pressure that will be reserved to allow for any contingencies such as air sharing on exit. In essence, each diver uses one-third of his or her gas supply before calling the dive. Using a full third is a best-case scenario and does not adequately take into account many contingencies. If I use one-third to penetrate the cave and my buddy has a catastrophic failure at the maximum penetration, we will have to remain in complete control in order to make it out alive.

As such, there are many scenarios when divers should reserve more than two-thirds for the exit of their dive. They include: Dissimilar tank volumes between team members, new cave, new gear, new dive partner, low/no flow, restrictions, complex navigation, siphons, tidal conditions, heavy traffic in cave system, and restricted exit.

To calculate thirds, a diver takes their actual pressure and rounds it down to the easiest value divisible by three. That number is then subtracted from the actual fill pressure. This builds in a little conservatism to the figure.

For example: If a diver has 2900 psi in their tanks, they would round down to 2700 and divide that by three. That makes 900 psi the useable amount of gas. They subtract 900 from 2900, giving them a turn pressure of 2000 psi. That means they use 900 psi to enter the cave and have 2000 psi to get two people out. This method works when both divers have the same size tanks.

Gas Matching

To account for dissimilar tank sizes, divers should compare actual gas volume in order to calculate turn pressure. The diver with the lowest volume is always the controlling factor, since a diver with large tanks may need to rely on the small ones to get out of the cave. There are many techniques for calculating dissimilar tank volumes. Here is one example:

IMPERIAL EXAMPLE

If Diver A uses double LP 104s with 2500 psi and

If Diver B used double aluminum 80s with 2500 psi

Then Diver B has a much smaller volume of gas.

By pure gauge estimates, Diver B would turn their dive at 1700 psi. In other words, they would use no more than 800 psi of gas.

That 800 psi can be converted to volume by multiplying by the tank baseline of .053, which gives us 42.4 cu ft. of gas. Diver B needs 42.4 to get themselves home form maximum penetration…. But…

If Diver A used straight thirds, they would need 800 psi to get home. But their 800 psi is actually a greater volume of gas. Diver A needs a volume of 63 cubic feet to get home safely.

Therefore either diver needs 42.4 + 63 cu ft. of gas to get both divers home safe. That total is 105.4 cu ft.

Diver A can therefore use turn their dive at a regular turn pressure.

Diver B with the smaller tanks must conserve extra gas for the bigger person and therefore use 133 - 105.4 = 27.6

Their turn pressure is calculated by dividing by their tank baseline of .053. Therefore, they may use 520 psi on the gauge and call the dive when it reads 2000 psi (always round up for conservatism).

METRIC EXAMPLE

Divers using the metric system often use a ratio method for comparing volumes and turn pressures.

If Diver A uses a 10 L tank and

If Diver B uses a 15 L tank

Then Diver A has 2/3 of the volume as Diver B

Diver A is the controlling diver.

If Diver A's tanks are filled to 210 bar, then they may use 70 and turn when their gauge reads 140 bar.

124

Diver B may only use 2/3 of the 70 bar or 46.6 bar before turning.

Here are two further methods to tackle the same problem:

METHOD #1

12 liter tank @ 240 bar	8 liter tank @ 240 bar
2880 liters	1920 liters
one third = 960	one third = 640

Use smallest third as penetration allowance.

Turns at 2240 liters	Turns at 1320 liters
2240/12 = 186 bar	1320/8 = 165 bar

METHOD #2 (when the small tank person has a very low SAC rate)

How much does each person need to get out?

960 + 640 = 1600 liters needs to be reserved for exit at a minimum

This diver uses 960	This diver saves 960 + 640 = 1600
80 bar (normal thirds)	She uses 1920 – 1600 = 320 liters
	320 liters/8 liter tank
	She can use 40 bar
	Turns dive at 200 bar

Many other modern aids are available for comparing dissimilar tanks. IANTD offers a series of charts in their *Encyclopedia*. Smartphone apps such as "Gas-Match" and "iDecoPro" or "V-Planner" assist with these calculations. Many personal dive computers also offer planning features. Whichever tool you choose to use, do so before hitting the water, so that mathematical errors don't leave you cutting corners on gas.

Respiratory Minute Volume

You should know how to calculate a figure known as Respiratory Minute Volume (RMV). This figure takes SAC rate and multiplies it by the depth, expressed in atmospheres, giving you an idea about how much gas volume you use in one minute at a given depth.

This estimate helps in the dive planning process and should be padded for conservatism, recognizing that regular consumption rate will change if conditions vary underwater. In a high flow cave, one may suddenly require a larger volume of gas that results in earlier turn time.

IMPERIAL: [depth (feet) / 33) + 1] = ATA

METRIC: [depth (meters) / 10) + 1] = ATA

Narcosis and Choosing the Best Mix

Now that mixed gas and appropriate training are readily available, most divers shy away from deep air diving and the nitrogen narcosis that comes with it. Most cave divers choose to operate with an Equivalent Narcotic Depth of between 100 - 130 feet, with ever more divers choosing the shallow end of the spectrum. This facilitates clear thinking and problem management in the most difficult scenarios. Even though a diver may believe that they are not impaired at depth, they will likely experience greater challenges in task-loaded scenarios when diving high partial pressures of nitrogen.

The EAD (Equivalent Air Depth) formula gives divers the ability to compare a given mix of gas to a theoretical depth equivalent for diving air. This figure may be used with air diving tables.

Beyond the depths of a standard full cave class (130 feet/40m), divers should seek mixed gas training, covering details about the relative narcosis of various inert gases and oxygen at greater depths.

Oxygen Planning and Choosing the Best Mix

It is important to plan for oxygen exposures, when selecting an appropriate gas for your dive. Historically, divers commonly used a partial pressure of 1.4 for the planned maximum operating depth of a given breathing gas and 1.6 as the maximum PO_2 for decompression gases. Cave divers and other technical divers have shaved back that level of exposure for increased safety and to be able to extend their dive. Most technical training agencies suggest 1.3 as the maximum PO_2 exposure for the bottom time and 1.4 to 1.6 for decompression, when the diver is at rest. CCR divers commonly use 1.2 for their bottom time and often for decompression. This takes into account the lengthy bottom times achievable on rebreathers and the fact that oxygen limits are easily reached. Additionally it pads a dive for conservatism since wet oxygen sensors may read slightly lower than an accurate reading if otherwise dry.

Oxygen planning needs to account for Central Nervous System (CNS) Toxicity and sometimes Pulmonary or Whole Body Toxicity. Open circuit cave divers will find that it is during their decompression that they net the majority of their

CNS time. CCR cave divers use a constant PO_2 so they take on oxygen equally on the dive and decompression.

It is important to keep track of oxygen exposure because a diver suffering from CNS toxicity may experience symptoms of visual disturbances, ringing ears, nausea, tingling, irritability and convulsions. Symptoms may not be detected before the onset convulsions and underwater convulsions almost always result in drowning.

NOAA O_2 Exposure Limits and CNS % per Minute Chart

NOAA has established single dive and daily limits for oxygen exposure. Simply look up the PO_2 in the left hand column to view the various limits.

A technical diver generally targets about 80% on the CNS Clock, or 80% of the value in Column 3 on the chart below. To calculate oxygen exposure for a single dive, use Columns 4 & 5. Look up the PO_2 at maximum depth or rebreather setpoint and multiply by the right column by the actual dive time to come up with the percentage on the oxygen clock.

Wrist computers track oxygen exposure at every stage of the dive. They accounts for depth changes and therefore arrive at a very accurate figure. When you plan for subsequent dives in the same 24-hour period, you can use the residual oxygen expressed in your wrist computer when forecasting the next dive with your decompression software.

O_2 Partial Pressure	Max. exposure for a single dive	Max. exposure for 24 hours		PO_2	CNS % per minute
0.6	720 minutes	720 minutes		0.6	0.14
0.7	570 minutes	570 minutes		0.7	0.18
0.8	450 minutes	450 minutes		0.8	0.22
0.9	360 minutes	360 minutes		0.9	0.28
1	300 minutes	300 minutes		1	0.33
1.1	240 minutes	270 minutes		1.1	0.42
1.2	210 minutes	240 minutes		1.2	0.48
1.3	180 minutes	210 minutes		1.3	0.56
1.4	150 minutes	180 minutes		1.4	0.67
1.5	120 minutes	180 minutes		1.5	0.83
1.6	45 minutes	150 minutes		1.6	2.22

Residual Oxygen Toxicity

After a long surface interval, you can calculate the residual percentage of CNS oxygen toxicity by using a half time of 90 minutes or greater. In other words, after 90 minutes, your residual oxygen toxicity percentage will be halved. In another 90 minutes it will be half again and so on. The following chart makes it simple to look up various surface interval times.

CNS Halftime Chart

CNS %	90 min	120 min	150 min	180 min	210 min	240 min	300 min	360 min
100	50	38	30	25	22	19	15	13
95	48	36	29	24	21	18	15	12
90	45	34	27	23	20	17	14	12
85	43	32	26	22	19	16	13	11
80	40	30	24	20	18	15	12	10
75	38	29	23	19	17	15	12	10
70	35	27	21	18	15	14	11	9
65	33	25	20	17	14	13	10	9
60	30	23	18	15	13	12	9	8
55	28	21	17	14	12	11	9	7
50	25	19	15	13	11	10	8	7
45	23	17	14	12	10	9	7	6
40	20	15	12	10	9	8	6	5
35	18	14	11	9	8	7	6	5
30	15	12	9	8	7	6	5	4
25	13	10	8	7	6	5	4	4
20	10	8	6	5	5	4	3	2
15	8	6	5	4	4	3	3	2
10	5	4	3	3	3	2	2	2
5	3	2	2	2	2	1	1	1

NOAA has further recommendations for the minimum surface interval between dives. Details on their recommendations for diving are provided free online by searching the search term "NOAA Diving Manual."

Calculating Pulmonary Oxygen Toxicity Exposure

In addition to CNS toxicity, cave divers should monitor their exposure to pulmonary oxygen toxicity, as known as whole body oxygen toxicity or the Lorraine Smith Effect. This is of particular importance to those on long expeditions or projects.

In order to track pulmonary oxygen exposure, Dr. Bill Hamilton developed a method called the "Repex Method," which uses a measurement called an Oxygen Toxicity Unit (OTU). These are calculated on single dives and accumulate after repetitive days of diving. Theoretically, staying within these limits should safeguard the diver from experiencing symptoms of pulmonary toxicity and still allow room for recompression therapy if it is needed. Use the following charts to gauge your exposure.

Pulmonary Dose

Partial Pressure	OTU per minute
0.6	0.27
0.7	0.47
0.8	0.65
0.9	0.83
1	1
1.1	1.16
1.2	1.32
1.3	1.48
1.4	1.63
1.5	1.78
1.6	1.92
1.7	2.07

Daily Allowances

Days	Daily Dose	Total Dose
1	850	850
2	700	1400
3	620	1860
4	525	2100
5	460	2300
6	420	2520
7	380	2660
8	350	2800
9	330	2970
10	310	3100
11	300	3300
12	300	3600

Time, Depth and Distance Planning

Using SAC rates, you can determine your projected bottom time. By taking SAC rate and multiplying it by the depth in ATA, you can project potential bottom based on available gas.

If a team determines that they can use 45 cu ft. of gas before turning the dive, and the highest SAC rate on the team is .6 cu ft. per minute and they plan to dive at Ginnie Springs in approximately 100 feet/30 meters (4 ATA) of water, then they will have the following limits:

45 / .6 = 75 minutes at 0 feet

75 min. / 4 ATA = 18.75 minutes at 100 feet before turning = 36-37 minutes bottom time

It can be summarized in the following way:

IMPERIAL EXAMPLE

a. The cave is _____ feet deep.

b. The pressure at depth is _____ ATA. [depth / 33) + 1]

c. My consumption at depth is _____ cu ft / min. [SAC x b]

d. My penetration time is _____ minutes. [useable volume / c]

e. My bottom time will be _____ minutes. [d x 2]

Once these factors are known, you can put the pieces together in a comprehensive dive plan. Computer and Smartphone apps do these calculations automatically, but it is important to understand how these figures are derived.

Final Planning

Once you enter the water, there are several final checks to complete before submerging. These are commonly referred to as the S-drill, or safety drill.

The first step involves a bubble check. A diver briefly submerges while their partner scans their equipment for leaks.

The second step involves checking all equipment from head to toe.

- Test second-stages while breathing them submerged.

- Check operation of backup lights in the water.

- Test drysuit and BCD power inflator. Feel for and check any pull dumps. Make sure the string is not snagged.

- Check reel(s). Ensure lock nuts are snug and that you have the right number for the dive plan. Ensure spools are properly clipped.

- Check that your computer is properly set or rebreather display working and set to correct PO_2.

- Check for presence and accessibility of all accessory gear including knife, markers, tables, slate or notebook, bottom timer and depth gauge, if applicable. Put your hand on each item for confirmation.

- Turn on the primary light and leave it turned on.

The third step in your final check is to establish gas turnaround pressures and review the dive plan. The team leader should walk teammates through the dive plan. Everyone should record his or her turn pressure and everyone should listen to ensure the calculated turn pressure is correct. Dive tables should be reconfirmed and the team should descend.

The final step in preparation is air-sharing rehearsal. In shallow water, divers take turns signaling "out-of-air" and practice breathing on their partner's long hose. This should be done in a hovering position. After contact is made, the partners can swim together while sharing air for a short distance, if space permits and visibility can be preserved. The drill is repeated until each team member has had a chance to both offer and receive air. This drill ensures the working order of all regulators, allows for good buoyancy and skill practice and confirms that long hoses are not buried under gear or entangled in any way.

Mixed Teams

When CCR cave divers and open circuit (OC) cave divers work together, they are referred to as a Mixed Team. OC divers are often reticent about asking a CCR diver about differing procedures. It is therefore incumbent on the CCR cave diver to ensure that gas management and emergency procedures are clear prior to entering the water.

Orientation

- Show how the rebreather is worn and how it can be removed from the diver if they become unconscious.

- Demonstrate how the wing is inflated and, if it is attached to an onboard cylinder, discuss how this limited supply could be easily exhausted during a rescue.

- Determine whether oral inflation of the wing by the buddy is possible.

- Discuss how developing problems can be quickly recognized.

- Demonstrate various warning lights, especially those that indicate life-threatening oxygen levels.

- Describe the significance of a vibrating mouthpiece, if applicable.

- Describe how and when it might be necessary to close the loop, and why preventing a loop flood is important for maintaining positive buoyancy.

- Practice sharing gas. Determine whether sharing a long hose or passing off a bailout bottle will work better.

Gas Planning in Mixed Teams

- Inquire about the SAC (Surface Air Consumption) Rate of the OC diver and plan appropriate gas volumes to ensure their safe exit using the rebreather diver's open circuit bailout gas.
- Select bailout gas that is compatible with the OC diver's decompression plans.
- Plan decompression gases to accommodate all emergency scenarios for either diver.
- Discuss whether the team stays together when they reach and complete decompression stops. The CCR cave diver will likely complete their deco much earlier than the OC cave diver. Will a diver be left alone to complete deco? If a CCR cave diver leaves early, will they be leaving any of their gas supply behind for the OC cave diver?

Complete a Modified S-drill

- The rebreather diver should describe what to look for during the bubble check.
- Rehearse gas-sharing scenarios before entering the cave.

   If CCR cave divers strive to maintain a high level of conservatism and independence with their bailout gas, then safety and flexibility are benefited. Self-rescue is assured and buddy-rescue of a CCR or OC diver is also probable. The goal of the orientation is not to teach the OC diver how to run a rebreather, only how to share gas and handle emergencies that may occur.

Other Mixed Teams

   Mixed teams are also created when backmount divers pair with sidemount divers. In this case, the S-drill will allow the divers to practice sharing gas. Additionally, each diver should familiarize themselves with the placement and operation of the wing inflator, which can be quite unique on a sidemount rig.

Gas Management for CCR Divers

   Catastrophic failures on open circuit scuba are usually manifested in events like high-pressure seat failure in a first-stage, hose rupture or manifold damage, burst disk and valve breakage. These failures are often accompanied by a "boom/hiss" that alerts the diver to a problem. Technical divers spend ample time rehearsing valve drills and exit scenarios, since gas loss equates to time pressure. They manage the emergency and get out quickly!

On a rebreather, failures more commonly develop slowly. In some ways, a hose rupture or first-stage failure is one of the easiest issues to deal with. In those cases, the diver simply reaches back, turns off the valve and feathers it on and off through their exit or they simply abort, using their open circuit gas. Other failures take time to manifest themselves on a rebreather and may do so without an alarm or visual clues for the diving partner.

In the early days of rebreather training, we used to put a considerable emphasis on keeping the diver on the loop. These days, we teach students the myriad options available to them in emergency scenarios, but encourage divers to bailout to open circuit if they have any doubt about the safety of what they are breathing, or if the task load is too large. If in doubt, bail out.

Examining the types of failures that could lead to the necessity of an open circuit bailout will help the diver choose how much gas they wish to carry.

Confusing Data

When the face of an oxygen sensor gets wet, it may read low and slow. Sensors that get wet on the wiring side may read high. If a diver has any doubt about their sensor readings, a vigorous flush with diluent gas will help them determine if any of the sensors are reliable and accurate. After determining which, if any sensors, are accurate, the diver may allow the system's voting logic to get them out of the cave if appropriate or run the unit manually with the single accurate sensor during the abort. If the diver is at all uncertain about the accuracy of their sensors, from flooding, age, poor calibration or other electronic failures, then an open circuit bailout is not just warranted but is the *only* safe option. We used to think that dual simultaneous sensor failures were unlikely, but there are several incidents and even fatalities where this appears to be the root cause. Sensors of the same age and physical history may fail simultaneously with another sensor of the same vintage.

None of the oxygen sensors in this photo can be relied on. The diver at 18 feet /5.5 meters has fully flushed their rebreather with pure oxygen and should see a PO_2 value of 1.5. In the event of three sensors disagreeing below this depth, the only option is open circuit bailout. Above 20 feet/6m, the diver can safely inject pure oxygen to accelerate their decompression and monitor their backup computer. Photo: Jill Heinerth

Catastrophic Loop Failure

Mechanical problems may cause catastrophic loop failures that demand open circuit bailout. Ripping or tearing a breathing hose in a tight passage, counterlung tears, dry-rotted rubber hoses, lost or torn mouthpieces and breakage of the DSV mouthpiece lever itself are all examples of failures that render the loop unrecoverable. In these cases, the CCR diver must bailout using open circuit gas.

Carbon Dioxide Breakthrough

Carbon dioxide issues are the most insidious problems leading to unrecoverable loop failure. Partial flooding may lead to channeling of scrubber material as will improper packing. Using carbon dioxide material beyond its intended specification may also lead to rapid breakthrough. Damaged non-return valves can also lead to rapid carbon dioxide build-up. Improper assembly such as leaving out a spacer or O-ring can also case rapid buildup that may not be detected in a pre-breathe sequence.

134

Given the scenarios above, I choose to carry ample open circuit gas to get myself out of the cave for almost all of my dives. I use at least two bailout tanks so that I always have one left if I give one away. I put a long hose on one tank so that gas sharing can occur via long hose rather than tank passing. In a few cases of extreme exploration, my team has opted to share bailout beyond a certain point of penetration. I find that carrying two, 80 cubic foot tanks in a sidemount style is very easy and comfortable and will get me out of most long dives. I use smaller tanks for lighter penetration. Beyond that, staged gas is preferred. Understanding that carbon dioxide issues will significantly elevate the SAC rate of an exiting diver, I am very conservative with gas planning. In some reports, the diver's SAC rate easily doubles and does not recover to a normal level during bailout.

Both IANTD and the NSS-CDS have adopted a standard for bailout gas, requiring that a dive team (three people) carry a minimum of 1.5 times enough gas to get a single diver out of the cave. Arguably, this results in greater team conservatism than is offered to open circuit divers in a pinch. However, it also leaves a team of three with the necessity to stay together and swap tanks throughout the exit so that nobody is ever left without some open circuit gas. Other divers have taken drastically different approaches. Some advocate a one-hour rule that gets any diver topside with one hour of any consumable in reserve, whether batteries, gas, scrubber or bailout.

My best advice to a rebreather cave diver is to make a careful risk assessment prior to your dive and visualize the worst-case possible scenario. Only then, can you make the right decision for you and your team about the amount of gas to carry in reserve.

The author using two bailout tanks mounted sidemount style with a PRISM2 rebreather. Photo: Mark Long

Gas Management for Sidemount Divers

Sidemount divers take care to balance the pressures between their two independent cylinders. Although sidemount divers still employ the rule of thirds, they have further reason to be more conservative than other configurations. Tanks should be kept within 200-300 psi of each other, requiring frequent switching of regulators. If the sidemount diver is traveling through small cave passages, they should realize that passage configurations or silting conditions might delay their exit more than a dive in large passage. Sidemount divers should consider using one or two long hoses on tanks to facilitate air sharing. A sidemount diver is considered to be capable of handling almost all gas emergencies on their own, however, having at least one long hose will make sharing with another diver much easier. There is never a scenario where giving up one of their two main tanks is advisable. Those tanks not only provide the basic gas supply but also critical ballast.

Decompression Theory

When cave divers reach the level of Apprentice Cave Diver or Cave Two, they will be engaging in decompression dives. Additional training in decompression procedures is recommended as well as training in oxygen administration and diving first aid. A complete education in decompression theory is beyond the scope of this text, but general concepts will aid divers in their understanding of different decompression models that are used by technical divers.

When a diver is under pressure, their tissues absorb inert gas. Different tissues absorb gas at different rates. Relative solubility varies between bone, fat, brain and other tissues. As such, the body is divided into theoretical tissue groups, known as compartments. The level of gas saturation within certain tissues is what controls a decompression model. When a tissue compartment becomes saturated, it reaches a level called "M-Value." Robert Workman of the US Navy Experimental Diving Unit (NEDU) first described the term M-Value. The letter "M" was intended to describe the "maximum" value that a tissue compartment could tolerate, without exhibiting signs of over-pressurization or supersaturation. Understanding the rate at which tissues reach supersaturation helps mathematicians develop models to predict safe ascent protocols.

Historically, divers relied on tables developed by military units around the world. The US Navy Decompression Dive Tables offered some of the earliest resources to divers. They were designed for single exposures, by young, fit soldiers using air for bottom time and decompression. This type of diving bears little resemblance to technical diving today and therefore, more suitable

136

models have been developed. New tables and computer software help a diver carrying a variety of gases, to plan profiles that better prevent DCS incidents.

In the earliest models, divers were encouraged to complete bottom time then rapidly ascend to a series of shallow decompression stops where they could sufficiently off-gas nitrogen or other inert gases. Profiles were very square. Studies over the last decade and more, seem to indicate that a slower ascent strategy with preventive deeper stops tends to help the diver off-gas more efficiently and prevent the growth of gas phase, rather than treating micro-bubbles in tissues at their point of supersaturation. This strategy of deeper stops also lessens the need for lengthy shallow stops.

Models such as Reduced Gradient Bubble Model (RGBM) and Variable Bubble Model (VBM) are popular decompression algorithms for technical divers. These models modify their ascent to a gradual curve with stops beginning deeper. Buhlmann tables have been modified using a concept called Gradient Factors, which permit a diver to select the degree of conservatism or aggressiveness of their profile. By determining theoretical M-Values, the model predicts when supersaturation will occur in different tissue compartments. The diver chooses how close they want to arrive at supersaturation at their first, deepest stop and how conservative they want the overall profile to be upon exiting the water. Erik Baker, an electrical engineer and computer modeling specialist, offers up many resources on the Internet that fully describe gradient factors in plain, easy to understand language. Google "Gradient Factors for Dummies."

Some computers permit the diver to select a personal gradient factor. Shearwater computers for example, set a default gradient factor of 30/70. What this means is that the deepest stop will be generated when the controlling tissue compartment reaches an M-Value of 30% of the way between ambient pressure and supersaturation. The rest of the stops slowly ease the diver up to 70% of the theoretical supersaturation level, in essence setting an exit conservatism of 30%, but with gradual off-gasing along the way.

In the Winter 2010 issue of *Alert Diver*, several noted experts weighed in on their opinions of deep stops. Generally, all agreed that divers can safely use computers and table models that already incorporate deep stops. They argue however, that any arbitrary adjustment of any diving algorithm may be very risky. Christian Gutvik, noted Norwegian researcher, reminds us that, "our current theoretical models and experimental results indicate that deep stops are beneficial only on longer dives."

Decompression Procedures

Training in decompression procedures is available from many agencies including IANTD, GUE, TDI, PADI, RAID, CMAS and NAUI. This training aids the diver in refining skills, and gives them background knowledge in using oxygen-rich decompression mixes and calculating decompression plans.

Cave divers should always have emergency oxygen available on site, whenever decompression dives are planned. It is a good idea to have oxygen-rich decompression gas in the water for any such dive. After any cave dive, it is wise to spend some relaxing time on the surface. This is called "surface decompression." At decompression stops, divers are often breathing 100% oxygen at depths as great as 20 feet/6 meters. At this depth, the PO_2 is 1.6, and off-gasing is very effective. Immediately upon surfacing, the diver's PO_2 drops to .21 and off-gasing slows. Divers should avoid strenuous exits. Lugging doubles immediately up a set of stairs, or carrying stage bottles out of the water requires heavy exertion. This extra workload could mean the difference between remaining asymptomatic and getting the bends. Surface decompression gives the body a chance to continue off-gasing prior to undertaking a heavy workload. Many divers believe that surface decompression should be at least half as long as the decompression time required at the last stop.

Decompression gases must be calculated separately from gas requirements for penetration. If the diver intends to use their back gas for decompression, they will need to reserve an appropriate amount out of their thirds plan. This amount must be enough to support two divers through decompression. For this reason alone, cave divers almost always place a decompression bottle in the water that has enough volume to support two divers, if needed. Decom-

pression cylinders must be properly marked for contents and maximum operating depth. If they contain mixtures that are richer than 40% oxygen, then the regulators and tanks must be oxygen cleaned at least annually. Improper care of oxygen tanks and regulators has resulted in death by explosion and fire, as well as numerous burn injuries.

An oxygen tank double clipped to your guideline in the cave can be easily found on exit, even in a silt out. It is preferable to connect your deco bottle to your own line rather than the permanent guideline where it may confuse or slow other divers in an emergency. Photo: Jill Heinerth

When a diver makes a gas switch, it should be observed by a partner diver, who visually traces the regulator second-stage back to the tank and confirms the appropriate marking and depth at which the switch is made. You can signal your partner when you are ready to switch and allow them to observe as you make the gas switch and reset your computer. Decompression tanks should be clipped to the line, pressurized, but turned off until they are needed.

Stops should be made as close to the required depth as possible, without creating any blockade to other divers who need to travel through the cave. Oftentimes, divers in a group may have different decompression schedules. They may have differing residuals from prior dives, may be utilizing dissimilar mixes or assorted gradient factors and computer models. As a result, stops may be generated at various depths for different team members. The team should plan ahead how they will manage this scenario. If one diver generates a deep stop, will the entire team stay at the stop or just within observation distance? If one diver clears all decompression obligations first, will they stay until the entire team has cleared? Although I never begrudge someone getting out of the water early, I would never leave a team member without the close observation of a buddy on decompression.

Emergency Procedures

Guideline emergencies have already been covered in Chapter 8, but there are a few other contingencies that a diver should be prepared to deal with.

Light Failure

If your dive light fails, your first reaction should be to swim to stay with your team. As you swim, visually reference or physically contact the guideline, if you are suddenly left in the dark. While swimming and maintaining trim, deploy your backup light and signal the team. Loss of a primary light requires that you abort the dive. During the exit, the diver using the backup light should be either placed in the center of the group of three divers or should be asked to lead out. They should never swim at the back of the group since their dive light may not be bright enough to gain the attention of the team.

Loss of Visibility

If the conditions are declining and visibility is suddenly lost, divers should immediately find the guideline and hold it with a loose okay sign letting the thumb close the loop by overlapping the fingertips. Touch contact should be established and the team should exit together. In most cases, silt-outs may only last for a short duration until reasonable visibility is regained and divers can return to visual reference of the guideline.

Gas Supply Emergencies

Gas supply emergencies are rarely completely catastrophic. In most cases, the failure of a hose may cause a sudden bang and bubbles. In this case, the diver should reach back and turn off the offending valve and use the functioning regulator to exit the cave. In some cases, first-stage high-pressure-seats will fail and result in over-pressurization and free flow to the second-stage. This situation is treated the same. Signal the team while shutting down the valve, and switch to a working regulator. If your gas supply is dwindling, use a buddy's long hose, but don't wait until you have depleted your tanks completely. Always leave some reserve in your own tanks to increase the available options. If a burst disk, manifold or tank-neck O-ring fails, you may need to isolate the tanks. In this case, turn off the manifold isolator, breathe from the leaking tank until it is depleted, then switch to the side you have preserved by closing the isolator.

Perhaps the most common gas supply emergency is a left valve roll-off. When your tank valves on back mounted doubles impact the ceiling of a cave, the left side will roll to the "off" position. This is one of the reasons that long hoses are generally mounted on the right cylinder. If a roll-off occurs and the diver goes to share air, they will pass a working regulator to the afflicted diver. When they put the short hose in their mouth and cannot breathe, they will immediately recognize the source of the problem and can reach back to correct it.

It is important for divers to have a solid mental blueprint of which hoses are served by each post of their manifold. Dry land drills that focus on trouble shooting different gas supply emergencies will help a diver visualize and manually react to a variety of problems that might occur.

When gas supply emergencies result in the need to share air, the donor deploys their long hose and switches to their secondary regulator, ensuring that the afflicted diver gets the regulator into their mouth. During this emergency, good buoyancy and horizontal trim are important to prevent silting. Using the guideline for visual reference, swim out of the cave in a rapid, but not exhausting pace. If a third team member is present, they will monitor the situation closely and switch out as the donor at a time reasonable enough to ensure a balanced supply and continued options for the team. If traveling through restricted areas, the recipient of gas should lead, so that the long hose does not get dislodged from their mouth. If visibility is lost, contact will need to be en-

140

gaged with the guideline and the buddy. The long hose may be routed through the hand that is holding onto the line for control and recovery if the second-stage is dislodged.

Stress and Panic

A little bit of fear is healthy, but stress can slowly erode sound judgment and awareness leading to perceptual narrowing and panic. When a diver is stressed, they lose control of their breathing first. As breathing rates elevate, respirations tend to become shallow. When ventilations are not full and functional, shallow breathing leads to carbon dioxide retention. In the presence of high levels of carbon dioxide, the breathing rate continues to rise, creating a feedback loop that retains more and more carbon dioxide. When a diver loses control of their calm breathing cycle, perceptual narrowing eventually leads to panic. As a result, the best thing a diver can do in the face of stress is to breathe in a relaxed and deep manner. Take a break, stop, breathe and think before acting. If you or a buddy is facing stress that is affecting your breathing or judgment, signal with your light, use the "hold" signal to take a break and/or call the dive.

Medical Emergencies

Cave diving can be very strenuous. Divers with underlying medical issues may suffer from a variety of conditions that result in very real emergencies for the entire team. Heavy workloads may contribute to heart failure or strokes. High partial pressures of oxygen may result in seizures, convulsions and subsequent drowning. Prescription medications may cause a variety of symptoms including seizure activity or unconsciousness in otherwise reasonably healthy individuals. Use of improper gas mixtures can lead to unconsciousness from narcosis, hyperoxia or hypoxia. Rebreather divers face additional risks of carbon dioxide poisoning, hypoxia, hyperoxia and caustic burn injuries, caused by wet scrubber materials. There are numerous situations that can occur well into a dive, leaving dive partner(s) in a position to manage a rescue.

Assisting an Unconscious Diver on the Surface

Unconscious divers on the surface should be given immediate, positive buoyancy and their airway should be protected from water. If the diver is close to the water's edge, prioritize getting them out of the water and into a position where you can "look, listen and feel" if they are breathing. If they are not breathing, then immediately give two, full, rescue breaths while pinching the nostrils and keeping the airway open. Once on the shore or boat, get into a position where you can check their pulse. If they do not have a pulse, then begin continuous CPR compressions. An emphasis is made on keeping the circulation going since oxygen is still in the bloodstream. Activate the emergency medical system (EMS) as quickly as possible. Continue to provide basic life support (BLS) through CPR and oxygen provision or rescue breathing if an ambulance is delayed. Keep going until a medical professional takes over.

First aid procedures are frequently updated as research better indicates the best practices. However, if you make any effort at all at resuscitation, then you can do no harm to a non-breathing victim who is essentially already dead.

Unconscious Divers Underwater

Very few divers who are unconscious and non-breathing in an overhead environment will survive. With this in mind, a rescuer must always consider their own safety during any rescue attempt. If a regulator or rebreather loop is still in the diver's mouth, try to keep it there to protect the airway. If it has fallen out, it may not be worth the time to replace it if you can ascend in very short order. If you are deep within a cave system when the emergency arises, your only option may be attempting in-water ventilation with the regulator while you move them horizontally out of the cave. With a rebreather loop, close the mouthpiece valve to prevent flooding, which can make victim very negatively buoyant. When you get to the point of direct ascent, suspend ventilation attempts, lift the chin to open the airway and carefully ascend while controlling both of your buoyancies. Place the heel of the hand on the regulator or BOV and finger tips on the mask to keep it in place, otherwise gas expansion will likely cause loss of the mask which may be providing some airway protection. On the surface, establish positive buoyancy, get them to shore, begin BLS and activate EMS.

If you are under a lengthy decompression obligation, you may elect to inflate the victim's wing to send them to the surface. If decompression is shorter, you may consider delivering them to surface support and immediately return to your decompression. In this case you should repeat some of the deeper stops and/or lengthen your entire decompression, as able. These choices are gut wrenching, since they inevitably involve a friend or even a life partner. These sorts of emergencies should be discussed before diving and must be a part of a full risk assessment and dive plan.

Since first aid recommendations are revised from time to time, you should remain current in first aid, CPR and oxygen administration.

Immersion Pulmonary Edema

Recently, attention has been given to a dangerous condition experienced by people immersed in water. This condition, called Immersion Pulmonary Edema (IPE) or Swimmers Immersion Pulmonary Edema (SIPE) may be under-diagnosed in the diving community. This author has now been the emergency provider in two cases and therefore I would like to share the background so that others can recognize contributing factors and presenting symptoms.

When my diving friend motioned for help beside our boat in Conception Bay, Newfoundland, I rushed to look over the starboard rail. He was gasping for breath with a rattling gurgle, pulling at his neck seal desperately trying to say , "I can't breathe!"

At the very stern of the vessel, I saw his dive buddy calmly moving onto the elevator platform, unaware of the issue. I immediately put the pieces together in my head:

- The victim was highly experienced with over 30 years of diving history.

- The dive buddy was unaware of the problem, yet they surfaced together on time. (Therefore I assumed they had completed deco and had a normal ascent).

- The victim was cyanotic, in extreme distress with rapidly worsening appearance.

I had a strong hunch that I knew what was going on and that getting him out of the water was the most important first step. I had seen this face before. A decade ago, I had a diving partner that suffered from this same malady.

The entire crew and passengers from our group of seasoned divers leapt into action. Within minutes, we had my dear friend seated on deck and were removing his dry suit neck seal and diving equipment. He coughed bloody froth into a bucket held by our sage Safety Officer. I turned to my diving partner, Cas Dobbin, and mouthed the letters, "I.P.E." His wide eyes affirmed my hypothesis. He nodded his head and I could see some of the alarm drain from his face. Oxygen was quickly fetched and the boat captain asked for instructions. I whispered to him, "have an ambulance meet us at the dock."

With the dry suit off and oxygen flowing, the victim improved rapidly. His skin color brightened and the raspy breath sounds were giving way to something resembling normal, yet labored breathing. He felt embarrassed and did not want to ruin anybody's day.

"You guys should go for another dive," he offered.

But the half-cup or so of pink, frothy spit was evidence enough that an emergency room was the best place to go.

Forty-two minutes after the dive, the victim was speaking well with good color. I shared my conjecture with him and he confessed to having had a similar incident more than a decade early. In that case, he improved so rapidly that no intervention was taken and his visit to the doctor the following week revealed undiagnosed hypertension. On this day, while swimming fairly aggressively at depth, in near freezing water, he felt fine but realized that he had forgotten to take his daily blood pressure medication. The dive essentially completed, he and his buddy began to ascend. It was at the bottom of the ascent line that he started to cough and experience difficulty getting a full and satisfying breath. Symptoms progressed rapidly but he did not even consider signaling his partner. He simply focused on breathing. With a full 17-minutes of decompression, he had to gather his wits and dig deep into thirty years of underwater resolve. When it was finally done, he surfaced at the bow of the boat and began pulling himself along the tag line to the stern. In the vertical position, with all the pressure of his dry suit pushing up around his neck, he got rapidly worse and signaled for help.

Sixty-two minutes after the dive, his breath sounded almost normal and he was able to walk off the boat to the ambulance. Exhibiting an oxygen saturation of 86% at this point, the medics continued him on oxygen and went to the local hospital where chest x-rays confirmed mild edema in the bottom of both lungs. The x-rays were not terribly remarkable, with dark patches low in the lobes, and the rest of the lungs appearing clear. Having seen a similar set of x-rays a decade earlier, I asked the ER doctor if she was comfortable answering a few questions. What transpired was an amazing collaboration between the victim, my buddy Cas Dobbin, an ER doctor, DAN, a hyperbaric specialist at the hospital and myself. 3D ultrasound and numerous other tools were used to qualify the diagnosis of IPE through exclusion of other issues.

By definition, IPE is a condition that can occur in anyone immersed in water, swimmers included. The process is not very well understood, but essentially, a swimmer or diver develops a cough, has difficulty breathing, develops a raspy breath and often coughs up frothy, bloody material from their lungs. It is reported in healthy, young individuals, triathletes, combat swimmers and the entire spectrum of the diving community. The onset can be very rapid or may develop over time and even over the course of a worsening cough each day. In medical speak, "during immersion in water, central redistribution of blood from the extremities occurs and is augmented when the water is cold. The resulting engorgement of the central veins, heart, and pulmonary vessels causes increased right-sided intravascular pressures."[1]

When an individual is unable to breathe, they often panic and can aspirate water and drown. They may skip decompression or ascend rapidly and concurrently experience decompression illness, aspiration, drowning and/or embolism. For this reason, and because the symptoms may also resolve rapidly on the surface (often before reaching the dock or hospital), it is believed that the syndrome may be under-reported and perhaps misdiagnosed. Sometimes labeled as a "panic attack" or ill-fitting gear, real cases of IPE may be completely overlooked.

Prevention of IPE

Studies have revealed that several external factors may create the perfect IPE cocktail including cold water, exercise, and high work of breathing. Numerous internal factors may also increase the likelihood of experiencing IPE including hypertension, cardiac issues, cardiovascular disease, and pre-dive hyper-hydration. Researcher Stefanie Martina cautions, "we see this in elite athletes too and not always in cold water. Don't rule yourself out. It can happen to anybody."

Treatment

Always eager to educate, Martina was clear about recognition and first aid. Basic symptoms include: inability to breathe, raspy breath sounds, and coughing up bloody or frothy sputum. Oxygen saturation is low, so oxygen administration is critical after rapid removal from the water. As long as someone is immersed, they may get worse, even if their head is out of the water.

Martina also wants boat operators and responders to know how important it is to listen to people about panic. Don't discount an event as anxiety and fail to recognize a serious physical malady. Anxiety could be part of a medical issue such as IPE and a trip to the hospital may reveal other underlying prob-

[1] Wester TE, Cherry AD, Pollock NW, Freiberger JJ, Natoli MJ, Schinazi EA, Doar PO, Boso AE, Alford EL, Walker AJ, Uguccioni DM, Kernagis D, Moon RE. Effects of head and body cooling on hemodynamics during immersed prone exercise at 1 ATA. J Appl Physiol (1985). 2009;106:691–700. doi: 10.1152/japplphysiol.91237.2008 and

Swimming-Induced Pulmonary Edema Pathophysiology and Risk Reduction With Sildenafil, Richard E. Moon, MD; Stefanie D. Martina, BS; Dionne F. Peacher, MD; Jennifer F. Potter, MD; Tracy E. Wester, MD; Anne D. Cherry, MD; Michael J. Natoli, M Eng; Claire E. Otteni, DO; Dawn N. Kernagis, PhD; William D. White, MPH; John J. Freiberger, MD, Circulation is available at http://circ.ahajournals.org DOI: 10.1161/CIRCULATION AHA.115.019464

lems such as hypertension and new onset cardiac conditions. 17% of sufferers experience more than one incident. Early diagnosis may help a diver or swimmer mitigate the contributing factors that could cause a subsequent attack.

At the hospital there may be little to do beyond supportive therapy and a search for contributory medical issues. Hyperbaric treatment is not used, and symptoms generally resolve completely with 24-28 hours. If you are awaiting attention in the emergency room, doing nothing beyond breathing oxygen, that may be exactly what is needed. The most critical aftercare will involve medical assessment by a physician (diving doctor if possible) who can rule out any other issues that need addressing before a return to diving.

Decompression Emergencies

Omitted Decompression

If a diver misses some of their decompression and surfaces early, there are a number of procedures that different organizations have developed as standard protocols. The US Navy, Comex, and other commercial diving operations and militaries have determined that, if the diver is asymptomatic, and can return to the water within five minutes, there are many options available. In some cases, the stops are repeated and lengthened by 1.5 times. In other cases, the diver descends one stop deeper than the stop they aborted and adds time all the way up. Several methods have proven successful, but are beyond the scope of this text. Whether the diver repeats stops, lengthens stops or stays out of the water, breathing oxygen after the dive will be beneficial. Even if the diver is asymptomatic, prophylactic oxygen may assist in off-gasing and prevent a full-blown case of DCI.

Decompression Illness

Decompression illness (DCI) is a very real risk for technical divers. Many minor hits are not reported or treated, and there is still an unfortunate atmosphere of secrecy surrounding DCI. Divers are embarrassed, and feel that getting bent reflects on their abilities as a diver. This could not be further from the truth. Technical divers push the edge of the envelope every day. Decompression tables are only theoretical mathematical models; fitness, age, gender and other factors may increase your likelihood for getting bent. Preventive measures may lessen your odds of getting bent, but there are no guarantees in technical diving.

Decompression illness is a term that describes both decompression sickness (DCS) and arterial gas embolism (AGE). DCS results from bubbles that grow within tissues, causing localized damage of one form or another. AGE happens when bubbles are injected into lung circulation, then travel through blood vessels, causing a blockage in blood flow. Both ailments are treated the same at the level of first aid and are thus often discussed in tandem. Both injuries result from a reduction in pressure surrounding a diver. In other words, the only way to prevent DCI is to stay down… permanently.

The longer you stay down and the deeper you dive, the more inert gas, such as nitrogen, is stored in your tissues until equilibrium is reached. The inert gas does not serve the body in any positive way, while oxygen molecules are used up as metabolic fuel. As long as you surface slowly, and according to a previously determined mathematical model, then in most cases, the extra inert gas will be slowly off-gassed as you come up. If you surface too quickly, or have other contributing factors, then the inert gas can come out of solution, forming tiny bubbles in the tissues and bloodstream. Bubbles that form in joints, causing pain, are associated with what is known as a "classic bend," but DCI has many other manifestations and complications.

Treating DCI

Signs and symptoms of DCI usually occur within 15 minutes to 12 hours after surfacing, with a good proportion of serious manifestations occurring within the first hour. Some cases are detected underwater or immediately upon surfacing and rare cases have been reported after lengthy delays, especially after flying.

DCI doesn't always hit a diver like a brick wall. It may creep up slowly and get worse. As such, denial is very common. Minor symptoms may be ignored as insignificant, but it also seems clear that an afflicted diver may not be able to make a reasonable decision for him or herself. Denial may be a symptom of neurological and chemical changes that are happening within the body and brain. It will be incumbent upon the dive buddy to take charge of the situation and arrange for treatment.

The only definitive treatment for DCI is recompression at a hyperbaric facility. But first aid can greatly improve the outcome of a diver. In some minor cases, oxygen may resolve symptoms completely, but a medical professional should make that judgment, since oxygen first aid may only delay symptoms for a while before they recur in a similar fashion, or even worse.

Immediately place a diver on oxygen and make a rapid assessment regarding the urgency of their condition. Oxygen should be provided at the highest concentration possible. Using a demand valve is preferred and saves gas, but a continuous flow mask with flow rate of 10-15 liters per minute may be used if supplies are abundant.

When symptoms are severe and onset is rapid, EMS must be activated immediately, since these patients will need to be medically stabilized before recompression therapy can begin. Divers Alert Network (DAN) should be notified early to facilitate communications between emergency physicians with hyperbaric specialists. Severe signs and symptoms may include:

- Severe and rapid onset of symptoms within an hour of surfacing

- Unconsciousness

- Worsening condition

- Difficulty breathing, dizziness

- Coughing

- Paralysis

- Stumbling and weakness

Careful monitoring of airway, breathing and circulation is important with an understanding that vomiting may occur.

Lay the diver on their side unless CPR is being administered. If aircraft evacuation is required, cabin pressure should be maintained close to sea level, so it does not exacerbate symptoms.

When the diver arrives at a hospital, medical staff will attempt to fully stabilize the victim. IVs are often established to rehydrate the diver and urinary catheters may be inserted for people who are having challenges with voiding. After stabilization, DAN medical staff can help arrange for evacuation to the nearest chamber facility. They contact the receiving chamber and relay medical information so that staff may be called to prepare the hyperbaric facility. Many chambers operate part time. Others are active in treating other medical conditions around the clock. DAN will find the closest option for rapid, appropriate therapy. They also standby for diagnostic assistance, and if necessary, make their own facilities available at Duke University Medical Center.

If you are accompanying your dive partner through medical evacuation, gather all the information you can about their dive, medical history and onset of symptoms. Few people other than medical specialists are able to adequately conduct and interpret a field neurological test, however, you can continue to monitor any changes in their status.

148

Many cases of DCS are less severe and may not require emergency transport. In these cases, the diver may be experiencing severe pain, especially in joints. The pain may be getting worse, but is progressing slowly over a period of hours. These divers should be immediately placed on oxygen and generous fluids by mouth to aid in rehydration. Calling DAN will help to make the decision about whether you can transport the victim or whether more urgent evacuation is needed. DAN will stay in contact as you travel to ensure that worsening symptoms do not require rapid intervention. The diver will, in most cases, still need to go to an emergency room for clearance, before being sent to a hyperbaric chamber. In some parts of the world, divers are accepted directly at remote chambers, but in the United States, emergency room stabilization, diagnosis and insurance authorization will usually come first.

As your dive buddy's advocate, you should ensure that DAN connects with the emergency room personnel as soon as possible. Let administrative clerks know that even though your dive buddy may be walking and talking, their condition requires immediate attention. Once in the emergency room, patients will usually be given an EKG and chest x-ray and may be placed on intravenous fluids with continued oxygen until they reach a chamber.

Some cases of DCS may be subtle. Signs and symptoms may appear vague and present themselves slowly over a period of many hours or even days. Many divers ignore symptoms for several hours, reporting their situation only when they are unable to sleep. That is why on-call staff organizes many chamber treatments in the early hours of the morning.

In mild cases, the diver may not even be sure if they have DCS. Call DAN for advice and direction. Report all diving activities for the previous 2 days. Describe all signs and symptoms, which may include strange rashes, pain, numbness, unusual niggles or other sensations. DAN medical staff will make a judgment call and likely advise you to go to a local medical center for evaluation. Hydration is important in all cases.

Leaving DCS untreated is unfortunately widespread in the cave diving community. Whether it is ignorance, embarrassment or denial, active technical divers will tell you that they know many divers who have ignored symptoms and resisted treatment. Sometimes symptoms subside on their own, but if the DCS is severe and untreated, a diver could be left with long-term disabilities, dysfunctions or muscle weakness. Spinal cord injuries may also result. More subtle cases, involving joint pain, may eventually contribute to arthritic conditions and degenerative disease like osteonecrosis.

Factors that May Contribute to DCS

There are numerous circumstances that may leave an individual more susceptible to DCS. Most factors call attention to the need for good general health and fitness, especially cardiovascular. Dehydration is present in most victims of DCS, though researchers have failed to call it causative. Dehydration causes fluid loss in tissues as well as electrolyte imbalance. Excessive sweating in warm climates, breathing dry gases, immersion diuresis, intentional dehydration to permit drysuit diving and general lack of fluid intake days before a dive, may cause it. Even though physicians suggest that dehydration is not necessarily a contributing factor to DCS, it is still a good idea to maintain good hydration. Other contributory factors include age, injury, illness, obesity, previous DCS hits, Patent Foramen Ovale (PFO), rapid ascent, omitted decompression, omitted safety stops, travel to altitude by plane or car, consumption of alcohol or drugs and heavy exertion during or after a dive.

Patent Foramen Ovale (PFO)

A PFO is an arterial-septal defect, which allows blood to shunt from one side of the heart to the other, bypassing lung filtration. When blood shunts from the right to the left side, it may carry micro-bubbles with it. These micro-bubbles can enlarge and pass directly into arterial circulation.

During gestation, a natural hole links the arterial chambers of the heart in the fetus. After birth, that hole closes and heals over when the baby begins to use its lungs. In up to one-third of adults, the flap does not heal fully and blood will shunt when increased pressure from coughing or exertion occurs. In diving, this allows venous blood, perhaps filled with micro-bubbles, to return directly to arterial circulation, bypassing the lung filtration and the opportunity to off-gas through normal breathing. Once in the arteries, bubbles may gang up and grow in size. These bubbles are more likely to cause neurological symptoms. They may block circulation to parts of the brain causing stroke, may lodge in the spinal cord, causing paralysis or may lead to heart attack.

Specialized physicians can test for PFOs by injecting gas into the circulation. While asking the diver to conduct a forceful Valsalva maneuver (ear clearing with pinched nose), they can look for bubbles on an echocardiogram. They may also ask the patient to do deep knee bends to further raise pressure.

Experts do not suggest that divers seek prophylactic testing for PFO, and many divers with aggressive diving activity and a PFO never get bent. That being said, given that one-third of divers may have some degree of shunting, it seems prudent to be very conservative about post-dive exertion that can raise pressure and lead to an opportunity for bubbles to move into the arterial circulation. This includes being careful about activities such as heavy lifting right after the dive. Recent research suggests that perhaps even the majority of people can experience either shunting or a bypass of bubbles from the lung filtration that can cause decompression stress or even DCI. This area of research is receiving considerable interest these days and as such, you should look for new information provided by reliable scientific sources.

Specialists, such as technical diver, Dr. Simon Mitchell, suggest that the event rate of severe DCS is still very low in people who have a PFO and those that don't have a PFO can still experience shunting. However, if you experience neurological DCS or frequent cases of skin bends, you may consider consulting a hyperbaric specialist that can discuss the risks and benefits of testing or repair.

Your Most Important Investment

DAN Insurance is extremely inexpensive. Having personally used their services, I cannot say enough about the excellence of this organization. If you take up cave diving, you simply must purchase DAN insurance. There are several different levels available from basic coverage to extensive additional travel insurance. Their website and magazine, *Alert Diver*, will help you stay current regarding advances in diving medicine. DAN's hotline is always available to answer non-emergency questions and facilitate treatment if needed.

The DAN Emergency Hotline number is **+1-919-684-8111 or +1-919-684-4DAN.** You will be connected with an expert in diving medicine. They accept collect calls from anywhere in the world and answer calls 24 hours a day. If your situation is not immediately life threatening, their regular number can be used.

Recovery Operations

There are few successful rescue operations in cave diving. When a diver is overdue, lost or suffers from unconsciousness in the cave, there are few happy endings. In these cases, recovery operations are initiated to bring the body out of the cave. The most important thing to remember is that the situation is no longer urgent. Care must be taken to protect others from harm. Patience will allow specialists to gather important information that may assist in accident analysis. Local law enforcement should be notified as well as the International Underwater Cave Rescue and Recovery (IUCRR). This network of volunteers works closely with law enforcement to organize safe and effective recoveries from overhead environments, including caves. Volunteers from around the world act as regional coordinators. A list of those individuals is provided on their website www.iucrr.org. By calling the regional coordinator in the area of an accident, a phone tree is initiated. The regional coordinator calls in qualified cave divers to assist in operations.

If you are on site when a diver is overdue, there are many important functions that you can fulfill. Search teams can be dispatched into the cave. Written records, with careful time annotations should be started. Dive partners may be interviewed for important information including time, depth and last location. Emergency equipment can be gathered at the water's edge in case it is needed. Backup tanks can be brought to the water in case a diver returns with insufficient supply to complete decompression. Divers not involved in the recovery should be kept clear from entering the cave.

On a long-term operation, an entire infrastructure may need to be built for the comfort and safety of search and recovery divers. Food, fluids, warmth and protection from the weather will all be important. Accident reports and witness statements should be provided to the regional coordinator and law enforcement as soon as possible to expedite the accident investigation.

The state of the victim's dive gear is extremely important in helping to determine the root cause of an accident. Trained recovery divers will carefully examine gear in place and post-recovery for important clues. Rebreather equipment is even more time sensitive to examine but should only be done so by experienced individuals. Examination of a CCR must be timely to be of significance since data can be lost when batteries are depleted. Changing anything on a victim's equipment is tampering with important evidence that may be used in either ruling out or highlighting equipment issues or operator error. The chain of custody must be carefully documented and should include observation by law enforcement personnel.

Training as a Recovery Specialist is offered at NACD and NSS-CDS workshops. The bipartisan organization, IUCRR, is supported by members of many agencies, law enforcement and other experienced public safety providers.

SPECIALTY
ACTIVITIES

CHAPTER 10

Specialty Activities --

CCR Diving

A diver plunges into a spring wearing his high-dollar technical rebreather. He slips into the water excited and eager to get into to the cave below. There is only one problem: he failed to turn on his gas supply. Meanwhile, across the globe another diver has spent her hard-earned money to get to a rarely accessed site. She readies her rebreather and finds that one of her oxygen sensors is acting strange. She decides to dive with her rebreather anyway. A third diver, worlds apart, prepares for a decompression dive. He has wisely chosen to purchase a rebreather to conduct this difficult dive. He has foolishly decided to forego carrying or staging adequate backup gas supplies, reasoning that a "lean and mean" assault on the site is a better idea. An abort, a rescue and a fatality occurred as a result of the above actions by divers. It doesn't matter who was involved or which was the worst error. Any one incident could have resulted in death.

These are real scenarios that have occurred in our community over the past number of years. As the popularity of rebreathers increases, incidents and accidents are on the rise. But as demonstrated through the events above, a community safety standard has not yet emerged. These days, divers can walk into a dive shop with a credit card and walk out with enough gear to get them to the end of almost any cave line on the planet. In some ways, this brings us back to the genesis of cave diving in Florida. It was a frontier filled with opportunity and few rules of engagement.

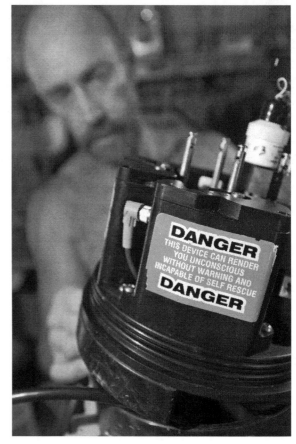

In the 1970s, cave diving pioneer Sheck Exley began to recognize patterns in the many fatalities that were occurring in caves. As a result, he authored the "Rules of Accident Analysis" (see Chapter Four) that have helped to educate divers since that time. In his *Blueprint for Survival,* he carefully analyzed cave diving incidents and fatalities and categorized errors in his list of Golden Rules for diving in the overhead environment.

The technical diving community lacks a similar code of conduct for rebreather diving. With rebreather companies and models changing about as quickly as Microsoft upgrades, it is difficult to address. However, in view of increased rebreather diving activity, especially in the overhead environment, it is a timely and important discussion indeed. Even considering the operational differences of various models, a basic list can be constructed. This list can be recalled with the simple memory device, "The Proficient Diver Fears Complacency."

Training

Several fatalities on rebreathers have been attributed to lack of training and proficiency. Divers need ample training on their unit and well-practiced emergency skills before taking on CCR cave diving. Considerable water time is needed to hone intuitive skills that are critical for rebreather divers. The diver is truly integrated into the breathing loop and needs time and experience to develop an intuitive link with their gear. If a diver is struggling with stress from task-loading or high flow, they may disregard a change in the pace of their solenoid valve or fail to question "that odd feeling" they are experiencing as a result of high carbon dioxide or low oxygen levels in their loop. Similar respect for training and currency is needed each time the diver learns a new unit.

Team practice is as important as individual rehearsal of skills. Photo: Jill Heinerth

Pre-Dive Checks

If you are not meticulous and diligent with pre-dive checks then you shouldn't consider owning a rebreather. Most manufacturers have developed stringent guidelines for pre-dive preparation of their rebreather. Generate a log page with a checklist that you can use every time you prepare your rebreather for a dive. A written checklist ensures that critical safety issues are never overlooked because of a momentary distraction. It also serves as a record of consumables and a diagnostic log that may aid in identifying developing problems with your gear.

A proper pre-dive check must include a pre-breathe sequence of five minutes, with the nose blocked. This should be done seated, while watching displays. A pre-breathe of this duration will likely catch many errors such as, carbon dioxide breakthrough, inoperative solenoid valves or failing to turn on your gas supply. Pre-breathing should never take place while you are walking to an entry or climbing/jumping into the water. You need to give full attention to your displays and equipment during this vital period. You should scroll through any display screens and check dive parameters such as your gas list, time, set point and auto or manual features.

Brian Kakuk carefully conducts his pre-dive checks in his shop in Abaco. Photo: Jill Heinerth

Decision to Dive

Pre-dive checks need to be conducted in an unhurried manner and without the pressure of rushing to jump in the water. Rebreathers require more care and maintenance than open circuit gear. It is critical that divers heed the warnings of a failed safety check. I have witnessed countless individuals who have elected to dive even though they have an errant sensor or a "small" leak. If you decide to jump into the water with a system error, you might as well place one foot in the grave. There is no dive that is worth the risk of starting with half of your options already used up. Complacency tends to creep into the routine of experienced divers who have logged repeated, incident-free dives. That same complacency has been a contributing factor in numerous fatalities to date.

Fitness

Since a rebreather is essentially linked with your physiology, it is critical that you be of optimum physical and mental fitness for diving. You must be able to recognize developing problems. If you feel anything unusual, you must be patterned to switch to open circuit or flush with appropriate fresh diluent to determine whether you have a problem. If the problem does not have an immediate solution, then you should remain on open circuit and get out of the cave. Only unquestionably diagnosed, solved problems permit return to the loop.

Contingency Planning

Backup planning is the lengthiest part of organizing a safe rebreather dive. It can be broken down into the following steps:

Gas Planning

Plan your onboard supply to accommodate all the depth changes you may experience during your dive. Frequent ups and downs in caves will require more diluent than you might normally anticipate.

Some rebreathers built today have significant onboard open circuit capacity, and a built-in second-stage suitable for open water diving. However, cave divers should not consider entering an overhead environment without adequate bailout gas to reach the exit and decompress.

Plan your open circuit bailout gas supply to accommodate the worst-case scenario of a catastrophic loop failure requiring an open circuit bailout all the way to the surface. This gas supply can be cached as stage bottles or carried by the diver. The "Alpine" approach to rebreather diving that fails to plan for catastrophic failures is foolhardy at best. A rebreather is not an excuse to cut corners in safety. If you cannot independently handle the gas needed for open circuit bailout and decompression, then you should incorporate support divers that can aid in caching an emergency gas supply. The only alternative to this approach is using a fully redundant dual rebreather with a completely redundant gas supply.

157

Decompression Planning

If your rebreather or decompression-planning tool is electronic, then you must be prepared with alternate plans for decompression. You should carry backup tables for open circuit bailout as well as Constant PO_2 tables or a back-up computer.

Rehearsal

Divers should practice critical skills for dealing with all possible failures. If you have an electronic rebreather, you should be comfortable with manual control in the event of a full loss of power. If you have rebreather with a sole-noid valve, you need to get in tune with the sound and pace of that valve and be ready to deal with all the possible failures associated with it. If there is any chance that a loop flood could cause a caustic cocktail, you need to envision how to deal with open circuit bailout, choking and alkaline burns all at once.

Team Planning

Dive buddies and support divers need to be educated about how to recognize and handle emergencies that may be specific to your rebreather. Open circuit divers need to be shown how they can access your gas in an out-of-air emergency. They need to be shown what your alarms indicate and how to switch to open circuit bailout. They need to know how to close your loop in case of unconsciousness. They need to plan their contingencies with consideration to the amount and type of open circuit gas that you are carrying.

A rebreather team of Terrence Tysall, Jim Rozzi and Tom Iliffe swim through Atlantida Tunnel in Lanzarote. Photo: Jill Heinerth

If team members intend to share the responsibility of providing adequate open circuit bailout gas – a technique I do not personally endorse – then consideration must be given to different buoyancy characteristics and unique clip systems on each other's cylinders. A rebreather diver that has to carry a tank that is out of trim may be jeopardized from making a quick exit. If bailout tanks are mismatched, then a long hose for air sharing may be a better option.

When the chips are down, the features of your rebreather are only as good as your ability to solve problems creatively and survive with or without those features. Make a set of laminated cue cards with all possible failure modes that your rebreather can present. On an open water dive, use the cue cards with your dive buddy to rehearse each emergency as a team. If you dive with an open circuit buddy, ensure that they know how to assist with any of those eventualities.

Finally, ensure competency in all emergency scenarios before diving in the overhead environment. It is wise for a fully trained overhead environment diver to log a minimum fifty hours in the open water before venturing inside a cave with their new rebreather. Rebreathers give us a gift of time to solve most problems. But it is unwise to push the learning curve too quickly and task load to the point of serious stress. Brand new rebreather divers tend to be very cautious. It is the diver with 50+ hours with no serious emergencies that tends to get complacent.

Rebreathers have opened a brave new world for underwater exploration and science. If used properly, they will open doors to discovery and adventure. So, if you have the desire for knowledge and the ability to be disciplined - go out and explore the world of rebreathers. If you are deliberate, patient and practiced you will do much, as long as you remember that the proficient diver fears complacency.

DPV Diving

Diver propulsion vehicles are gaining popularity like never before. Whether divers are motivated by the speed or the extension of range is personal, but DPVs in caves require additional experience and training. Specialty courses are available through experienced cave diving instructors and some sites will require proof of cave DPV training in order for you to use a DPV on their property. Many private and state-owned properties have an outright ban on scooter diving in order to augment site conservation.

The author driving the Thin Man scooter at Wakulla Springs. Photo: Richard Nordstrom

You should learn to use a scooter in the open water before entering a cave. The first step is to prepare an adjustable tow cord that can attach the scooter to your crotch strap D-ring. This adjustable length line should be carefully lengthened or shortened until you are able to easily reach the throttle handle with a bent elbow without stretching or overreaching. You should never strong-arm a scooter, since fatigue will be almost immediate. It should pull you easily. Ideally, your outstretched arm will rest on the throttle and a slight flex of the wrist will enable motion. You should carefully adjust the scooter for neutral buoyancy and horizontal trim to avoid fatigue. This is done with the attachment of very small weights inside the housing either weighting the nose or the engine end for proper trim. Slightly larger weights will be used in salt water.

Your gear will need careful examination for trim. The prop wash will tend to run across your hip and down your leg. Anything in the way of the prop wash will hamper speed and efficiency. A dangling second-stage will purge in the wash.

Helmets are essential for protection in a cave, and they allow a diver to mount lights if desired.

Before using a scooter to reach a particular destination, you should swim there to learn the terrain. In the event of a failure, you must be able to swim back, so you better find out if you are capable of making the distance. If you can't swim back, you need a backup scooter.

When planning your turn time, gas supply or bailout, you need to account for a full-penetration swimming exit. Some people choose to calculate sixths for this purpose, but it is more realistic to look at conditions and make a safe plan that covers you and a buddy. Figure out your SAC rate when being towed. Figure out how much the flow will affect your exit. Because this type of gas planning requires a lot of experiential learning, DPV use should be limited to cave divers with lots of time and training under their belt information is gathered slowly through progressive penetration dives.

Tow-behind scooters are more popular in caves than ride-on DPVs. They are easy to drive in a streamlined fashion and keep the prop in the diver's field of view. Propellers are notorious for sucking up and entangling gear, so clean trim and well-stowed equipment is essential. Divers may carry a dedicated tow strap or plan on grabbing your buddy's crotch strap if you need a tow. The tow strap will be much more comfortable for long distances and will aid in stream-lining.

Among other skills, you will complete the following drills during your Cave DPV class:

- trim, weight and rig a scooter
- gas planning for DPV diving
- adjust a tow line/strap on a scooter
- tow a disabled scooter and/or a buddy with a disabled scooter
- swim with a disabled scooter
- tie off a broken scooter
- disable a runaway scooter
- air share while driving a scooter
- using reels and spools with DPVs
- navigating restrictions
- using stage bottles with a DPV
- charging, care and maintenance of a scooter

Beyond diving skills, a DPV pilot needs to be a bit of a mechanic. Scooter batteries must be burn-tested and motors need minor maintenance. Online resources and manufacturer's guidelines will direct you to more in depth materials regarding your particular DPV.

Survey Techniques

Underwater cave survey is an advanced skill that comes with significant task loading. You may be surprised to discover the magnitude of effort that goes in to creating a detailed underwater cave map. However, if you are an explorer, you will need to be at least somewhat literate in basic survey techniques, because your exploration won't be recognized if survey data and a map do not accompany it.

Brian Kakuk surveys Freshwater Cave in Christmas Island. Photo: Jill Heinerth

Traditional Techniques

Traditionally, a knotted line is laid through the underwater tunnel and periodically tied to projections on the walls, ceiling, or floor. The surveyor's task is to take measurements at each bend in the line, consisting of, the depth on the line, the azimuth (compass bearing) of the line leading to the next station, and the distance to the next station. The distance is estimated by counting the knots (which are tied at uniform intervals, typically 10 feet, 3 or 5 meters) and estimated between knots. These, along with estimated passage widths, heights, and floor depth, and sediment details are recorded on a slate or in a notebook. This procedure is time consuming. Limited time restricts detail.

Step One - Planning

Site Selection

If you are embarking on your first survey project, keep things very simple. Find a location that has the following characteristics: shallow, low flow, warm water, silt-free and limited in scope. Exploration survey on the other hand is always a surprise. We rarely have the luxury of selecting ideal conditions in exploration. The very fact that you are moving through an unexplored passage means that you are likely encountering plenty of percolation from the ceiling. If you are exploring in North America, many of the best booming boreholes have been scooped. You are likely sidemounting in less than optimal conditions with low, silty corridors while dealing with chilling temperatures.

Dmitri Gorski practices survey technique with his buddy in The Catacombs at Ginnie Springs. Photo: Jill Heinerth

Team Planning

The commitment of the team will dictate what kind of survey is achievable. Many teams doing their first survey project get a little over-excited and think too big. Pick something achievable and get serious commitments from individual members. Expect attrition. People get busy, bored and sometimes lose interest in the project. Have backup personnel ready to step in to complete the job. Reading John Burge's, *Cave Survey* book, you will see that his first survey project in the Ginnie Ballroom was an enormous undertaking that took years to complete.

Survey Proposal

At this stage, plans are made for the techniques that can be applied. Based on the actual site you may need to employ various diving techniques including staged decompression, sidemounting or no-mounting. You'll need to predict what is achievable considering the talents and backgrounds of the team. Surveying is task loading in and of itself. It is not a good idea to turn survey dives into training or practice dives for new techniques. Be competent with your skills before embarking on a survey.

Individual Dive Planning

Once a master plan is made, individual dive plans can be arranged. The larger goal is divided into small achievable segments. Specific objectives are set for each dive and specific tasks are assigned to each individual. Dry runs can be conducted as rehearsals. At this point it is also important to get commitments not just for dives but also for cartography, drafting, landowner logistics and other tasks that need to be completed.

Rehearsal

Before a team can survey together, they need to dive well, together. A tight team that can communicate effectively underwater will do a more efficient mapping job. Safety should be the first consideration in any plan. Task loading can create a danger for people trying to accomplish too much in one dive. Beware of goal-oriented dives, which force people into the mind set of - "Oh, just more station to complete, even though I have exceeded my air turnaround time." Time pressure is an important consideration. If you are surveying on the way out of a cave, it will take considerably longer than laying line on the way in. Be vigilant watching air pressure and decompression obligations. It is ideal to survey on the way in, when visibility is better, and the dive can be called at an appropriate time. Data can be checked through back-sights on the way out, if time allows.

Step Two - Equipment

Slates and Notebooks

Used for data gathering, this is a critical piece of equipment that you will customize to meet your personal needs. A survey slate has: pre-inscribed information, a compass, bubble level, optional depth gauge and attached pencil(s). The bubble level is extremely important for ensuring accuracy of compass bearings. Remember to use non-magnetic, mounting hardware when assembling your slate - stainless or brass. Some people also carry a pencil sharpener and eraser with this kit and absolutely a spare pencil. I like to drill a hole through a small eraser and skewer it with the string that secures the pencil to the slate. I have found that these erasers last for years. Multiple slates in the form of Wet Notes books or Dive Rite Executive Slates can also replace the slate. You'll need to rule lines for as many stations as you anticipate in the dive planning process.

Preliminary notations on slates should include at least:

- Station Number
- Depth at Station (depth measured on the line)
- Distance between stations
- Compass bearing (azimuth)
- Remarks (additional shorthand notes discussed later)

Brian Kakuk carries a fiber-glass tape and survey slate while working on a deep cave off the Bermuda Bank. Photo: Jill Heinerth

Reels

Plan the length of line for the survey dive objective. Use knotted line with low stretch coefficient. Line cutters are often mounted on the handle of the reel or on the wristband of a computer for easy access. Some surveyors use rope counters for better accuracy. However, it is still a good idea to knot the line for future reference. It is considered shoddy practice to lay line that is not knotted. It is also understood that if your work is not surveyed - then you really haven't been there.

Fiberglass, surveyor's tape measures are used for the most accurate survey of distances. These reels are operated station to station, with a diver on the reel end, and a diver at the bitter end, also known as "dumb end," of the tape.

Markers

A slate that indicates that the cave is being surveyed should be placed at the cave entrance where people are likely to tie off. Sometimes signs above water are also posted. Leave a message that says something like, "Please don't disturb the lines or markers within the cave - survey in progress."

When a highly accurate survey is being produced or when a survey will take more than one dive, then markers are placed at each new station. Small, numbered slates or line cookies can be left so that future surveyors can reference the same locations easily.

Line arrows with distances from the nearest opening can be placed in the cave as the survey progresses. While working on the project, blank line arrows or color-coded line arrows can be used for directional indicators, or to indicate leads that need work.

Compasses

If mounted on the slate, a compass must parallel the edge of the slate precisely. The slate is held against the line when the azimuth is read. If you are right handed, mount the compass on the left side of the long edge of the slate. Remember not to use magnetic hardware. Check your screws by holding them by the compass; ensuring the needle is not affected. Compasses need to be calibrated when more than one is used for a survey. Choose a master compass in the group and compare other units to the master. Each diver can be given an error factor that should be applied to his or her figures to calibrate everything to the highest accuracy. Digital compasses are now included in many high quality dive computers. Most of these are accurate but should also be calibrated for a particular location before diving. Many of these types of compasses have a "time-out" feature that can be frustrating as you switch between azimuth and depth. Several buttons pushes may be required to move around the data, so rehearse topside, so this can be achieved in minimal visibility, while affected by narcosis.

Depth Gauges

Digital computers are ideal. If you do not have a computer or digital depth gauge, then a standard depth gauge with fine delineated markings can be used. These must also be compared with the devices belonging to the rest of the team. A master depth gauge is selected and everyone else must add the margin of error to his or her calculations. Ensure everyone is set on the same fresh or saltwater setting.

Helmets with Lights

These are critical for survey work because they keep your hands free for using the slate and writing notes. Exploration survey is often completed in almost zero visibility, caused by percolation. Head protection is important. When mounting lights you can use commercially available light holders or make your own specific ones with PVC pipe pieces or bungees. Design a mounting system that allows for removal of the light underwater.

When mounting lights on the helmet, angle the left light downward so it illuminates the slate or notebook. The right light can point forward for viewing the cave. Some divers mount GoPro camera to the helmet to aid in survey and refresh the memory for later sketching.

Lights

High intensity HID and LED lights are ideal for illuminating enormous passages, but a small hand or helmet-mounted light is worth its weight in gold. You need to use two hands to survey and therefore need a hands-free light.

Lights and all survey equipment should be carefully stowed with attention to trim. You will need to deploy items with one hand, in zero visibility. You also need to protect detailed notes made in pencil during the exit.

Step Three - Gathering Data

Laying Line & Station Selection

It is ideal to run the line on the floor and not zigzag up and down, ceiling to floor. Leave room for the surveyor to get directly above the station point with slate and compass in hand. Sometimes tempting wall tie-offs do not have room for a diver to properly view a compass from above or through the sight. Keep the line out of the flow so it does not "bend" or curve. Try to keep stations as level if possible. It is difficult to get an accurate azimuth if the line is slanting up or down.

Measurements

Hold the slate level against the line. Try to be as accurate as possible. 5° readings are not precise enough. You should be patient and aim for 1-2° if possible. Avoid parallax errors by looking directly down on the compass or by looking horizontally through the sighting window. This is the weakest link in the system - human error, rushing to read the azimuth.

Line depths at stations must be recorded, and only measure ceiling and floor depths if you have extra time. You can always follow up on another dive.

Count knots and estimate distances, or use a fiberglass tape. When using a tape in limited visibility with a partner, pull signals must be established. Rebreathers are a great tool for survey team communications since voices travel effectively.

Another technique for measurements is to cut a length of line about five feet long. This length can be managed by the surveyor using outstretched arms. Mark increments on the rope with a Sharpie waterproof marker. The surveyor can measure a long stretch of line by moving down the line in an "inchworm" technique moving hand to hand. Some cavers in Mexico call this the "ropey-dope" technique. It is very effective and can be done without assistance of another diver.

Notations and Sketching

Walls, features, and cross-sections should be sketched from a viewpoint relative to a normal diver's position within the cave. Survey notes should also indicate whether azimuths and sketches were taken inbound or outbound.

Bil Phillips guides Kenny Broad in the preliminary stages of surveying a cave on an expedition in Cuba. Photo: Jill Heinerth

Step Four - Drafting

XY Line Plotting

Using graph paper, protractor and ruler, you should plot basic XY coordinates as soon as possible after the dive while your memory is still fresh. It is amazing how cloudy your recollections get the day after a dive. I suggest transferring your personal data first and then discussing the details with your dive partner later. Your buddy can offer confirmations on your notes. Plotting these figures in a computer program such as "Compass," will make the mathematics easier and lessen sketch errors.

Outer Boundaries - After plotting the line path, wall sketches can be drafted, roughly indicating the placement of the line within the tunnel and the width of the passage. Obviously this will take extra dives.

Cross-sections - If a high-grade of survey is attempted, cross-sectional sketches can be marked on the evolving map.

Features & Details - Once outer wall boundaries are sketched, you can add features like pits, boulders, and breakdown piles.

Classifications of Survey

The British Cave Research Association has designed standards for accuracy of cave maps. The following standards were outlined in, *Cave Surveying,* July 2002.

BCRA gradings for a cave line survey:

Grade 1: Sketch of low accuracy where no measurements have been made

Grade 2: May be used, if necessary, to describe a sketch that is intermediate in accuracy between Grade 1 & 3

Grade 3: A rough magnetic survey. Horizontal & vertical angles measured to ±2.5°; distances measured to ±50 cm (6 inches); station position error less than 50cm (6 inches).

Grade 4: May be used, if necessary, to describe a survey that fails to attain all the requirements of Grade 5 but is more accurate than a Grade 3 survey.

Grade 5: A magnetic survey. Horizontal and vertical angles measured to ±1°; distances should be observed and recorded to the nearest centimeter and station positions identified to less than 10cm.

Grade 6: A magnetic survey that is more accurate than grade 5, (see note 5).

Grade X: A survey that is based primarily on the use of a theodolite or total station instead of a compass.

Note: It is almost impossible to attain a Grade 3 survey underwater.

BCRA gradings for recording cave passage detail:

Class A: All passage details based on memory.

Class B: Passage details estimated and recorded in the cave.

Class C: Measurement of details made at survey stations only.

Class D: Measurement of details made at survey stations and wherever else needed to show significant changes in passage dimensions.

Notes:

1. The accuracy of the detail should be similar to the accuracy of the line.

2. Normally only one of the following combinations of survey grades should be used:

1A, 3B or 3C, 5C or 5D, 6D, XA, XB, XC or XD.

Step Five - Confirmation

Notes are now transferred to a permanent record sheet. Information is expanded. Mathematical corrections for distances and depth are made using trigonometry.

Depending on the grade of survey you are working towards, it may take several dives or years to reconfirm data, measurements and sketches. Additional notations may be added. Check to see if you have achieved the loop closure that you seek. Loop closure means that if you are surveying a looping side passage, the survey joins successfully at the first/last station. Otherwise, re-dive and redraft and consider surveying in the opposite direction for a fresh outlook and chance to find mistakes. Computer programs close hanging loops and calculate the degree of error that occurred through closure. Software is designed to average errors and distribute them through the path.

Step Six - Cartography

Scale Selection

If this map is ever to be enlarged or reduced, it is better to make a relative scale bar rather than an absolute scale such as "one inch equals 5 foot." It is advisable to show imperial and metric or at least the locally appropriate measurement scheme. Cross-sectional sketches may have their own, different indication of scale.

Layout

Drafting vellum is a useful tool for tracing. Use Cartesian coordinates as opposed to relative coordinates to the last position to lessen cumulative errors. Ideally, you should assemble the following tools for the job: drafting table with smooth vinyl cover, pencils, pens (Rapidograph permanent), engineers drafting set with rulers, dividers, and protractor, lettering templates (Leroy), eraser & Xacto blade. Otherwise, head to your keyboard and input the figures into your mapping software spreadsheet.

Notations

Your map should be detailed with the following notations: legend, scale, compass rose, border and title. The title includes: name of cave, county, state, country, date of survey, names of survey team members, USGS Survey Spring ID Number (if there is one), grade of survey as per BCRA, total length of survey, penetration from the entrance, notations if there is more than one exit, names of original explorers, draftsperson's names, legend describing symbology, and copyright information. A good map will include a plan view, cross-sections and profile.

Publishing and Copyright

Copyrights are available for published and unpublished work. Copyright allows the owner to reproduce their work, to prepare derivative works based upon the copyrighted work, distribute copies of the copyrighted work to the public and to display the work publicly. Your map representation may be copyrighted but not: titles, slogans, designs, ideas, methods, systems, processes and concepts. The info on the map is not protected, but reproductions, display and distribution are protected.

Copyrighted material must bear the copyright mark. Unpublished works should have the © symbol, year and your name. Current info on copyrights can be obtained from the Copyright Office, Library of Congress in Washington, D.C.

The Next Millennium of Exploration and Survey

Wakulla Spring is one of the great springs on our planet. Members of the Narvaez and de Soto expeditions of 1528 and 1539, respectively, were presumably the first non-native persons to view the spring. Located 20 km south of Tallahassee, Florida, the spring erupts from a great funnel beneath a basin, 300 feet in diameter, giving rise to the Wakulla River. It is a first magnitude spring, and yet the source of the water remains fully undescribed, but proba-

170

bly part of a vast, complex, subterranean aquifer underlying a large portion of northwestern Florida. The spring is a window into to the health of the Floridan Aquifer as it becomes affected by logging, pollution, and urban expansion.

In 1998, Dr. Bill Stone launched an aggressive campaign to create the first accurate 3D map of cave. Well before its time, the Wakulla Mapper detailed the tunnel geometry to an incredible accuracy of 15 mm. This data, replayed in 3D to scientists, provided a never-before-possible means to study and appreciate this natural wonder. The mapping unit contained a high resolution onboard Inertial Measurement Unit (IMU), based on a laser gyro platform for determining the position and attitude of the system relative to an inertially defined cradle in the spring basin. By itself, this system acquired coordinates sufficient to reconstruct the three-dimensional vehicle trajectory through the cavern tunnel; in essence, a line survey. However, the mapper took a significant step beyond this level by incorporating a side scan sonar system. The sonar array fired a pulse and received the reflected signal, 4 times per second in 32 directions around the barrel of the unit. The objective was to log sonar data at 5-degree intervals. Given that the vehicle had a speed of roughly 200 feet per minute, this represented a significant data stream. To handle the data, the onboard system contained a storage processor equivalent to eight super computers. On one mapping mission, my partner and I obtained a 9.5 mb file, which was highly compressed. The result is a stream of three-dimensional points, which define the walls of the cavern tunnel along with a vehicle trajectory path

through the middle, representing the actual flight path taken by the diver. The data appears as a point cloud, or a series of dense spots painted on the walls of the cave, with a representation of a guideline down the center of the spiral of data. The final step following a mission is to download this information to a workstation where, through the use of polygons, it is possible to create a near realistic reconstruction of the interior of the cave.

The author prepares to enter the water at Wakulla Springs on an exploration dive. Photo: Patty Newell Mortara

171

The mapping system is remarkable because it is capable of operating in zero visibility. During our three-month project in 1998-99, we experienced the full gambit of visibility at Wakulla. Many of the passages in A/O Tunnel - the main tunnel at Wakulla - are well over 100 feet wide. Many of our dives in that passage were conducted in 20 - 30 feet of visibility or less. What that meant, is that for literally hours of scooter driving, we rarely saw the floors, walls or ceiling. We were glued to the tannic stained line as we motored along. When we returned from these dives, it was inspiring to see the data unfold before us. Not only could we see the walls, but also unexplored side passages, in glorious accurate detail.

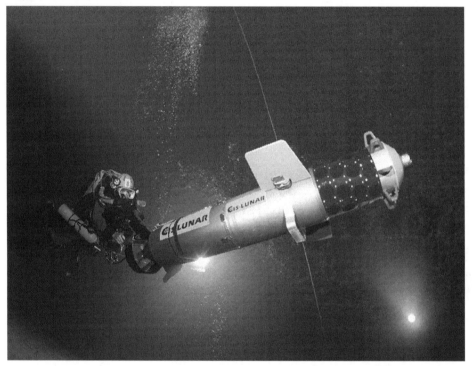

Dr. Bill Stone's Wakulla Mapper driven by the author. Photo: Wes Skiles, Courtesy of the U.S. Deep Caving Team Inc.

The next step in refining our survey included using "Cave Radio." We carried a series of ULF radio induction coils into the cave. The earliest rendition of these beacons was hula-hoop-sized magnets connected to a battery pack and timer. We strapped the coils to our scooters, and transported them to critical junctions within the cave. At approximately 500-foot intervals, we deployed coils as waypoints. We leveled them on the floor of the cave with a bubble level and activated the battery pack. We then secured the toggle with a wire stop so the pack would not inadvertently turn itself off under the 10 ATM pressure.

The coil was set on a time delay so that our radio expert could home in on the signal at the "quietest" time of day. He regularly consulted weather forecasts to ensure that he was staying away from times with high interference from approaching storms.

Once the radio coil was activated, our expert, Brian Pease, would hit the field with his boots and machete or canoe and paddle and seek out the signal. Once he found it, he would place a stake in he ground and return later with the GPS Total Station to tie into satellite data. Brian's detail-oriented approach allowed him to zero in to within inches of the location.

Once these locations were registered on the surface, we left permanent reflective floating beacons in the cave. Each time that we flew over the markers with the mapper, we would hit a waypoint trigger to register the known point. With this data, we could correct the drift errors every 500 feet or so.

It goes without saying that this had never been done before and that the ramifications extend far beyond Wakulla Springs. An accurate surface location to the mapped tunnels allowed for a new means of studying the countywide hydrology surrounding Wakulla and the city of Tallahassee. We could literally walk people over the surface and show them exactly where the tunnels lie beneath the surface. It will be possible, for example, to visually interpret the significance of surface features, however slight, relative to the underlying conduits. These same data, because they provide an accurate three-dimensional representation of the cave passages, can be used to establish flow models for simulation of spill and pollution control techniques. If an oil spill occurred at nearby St. Marks, we could determine whether the spill would seep directly into the aquifer. Scientists could use flow analysis to determine when the contamination might be seen in the aquifer and at what concentration and time it would appear in the spring itself. Most importantly, scientists and planners can better establish what areas are in need of proactive protection.

The author drives the Wakulla Mapper, leaving behind the transfer capsule for the decompression habitat. Photo: Wes Skiles, courtesy of the U.S. Deep Caving Team Inc.

173

This technology has gone far beyond the limits of Wakulla Spring. The Wakulla Mapper has morphed into a self-swimming, autonomous 3D mapper, capable of not only mapping, but also grabbing samples and other scientific evidence along the way. Tested in Antarctica and Alaska for several seasons, the mapper may be the first visitor to Jupiter's Moon Europa, where it is proposed to dive deep into ice-covered oceans to map and detect life in outer space. This same system is capable of autonomously mapping a cave system.

Cristina Zenato uses a device built by Sebastien Kister that measures line and tracks depth at survey stations (above). Dr. Bill Stone's Sunfish Mapper makes a trip into Peacock Springs where the artificially intelligent robot was able to map the cave in 3D in staggering detail in late 2016 (below). Photos: Jill Heinerth

Women's Issues

Risk of Decompression Illness

Although there are still a statistically small number of women divers to compile an accurate picture, it appears that women of equal experience and physical condition face an equal risk of suffering from decompression sickness as their male counterparts.

After reading many articles and attending seminars, my interest in the topic of women and decompression illness (DCI) was peaked in the spring of 2000 when I personally experienced the bends. Diving with my husband during a deep cave expedition, I suffered a hit when he was without symptoms. Luckily, my case was not too serious. My symptoms included pain, inflammation and soreness associated with Simple DCI, but also minor numbness in the arms, which is associated with Type 2 or Neurological DCI. Regardless, I wanted to fully understand the circumstances that may have contributed to my incident.

Dr. Jolie Bookspan, in her book *Diving Physiology in Plain English,* states, "there is no conclusive difference in physical susceptibility to DCS between men and women."

At a DEMA Workshop about Women and Diving, Dr. Maida Taylor of Diver's Alert Network (DAN), described that most accidents for women occur when they have been diving for less than one year, have fewer than 40 dives and are mostly open water divers. I certainly didn't fit that mold. However, she went on to describe that although we are no more likely to get bent than our male counterparts of an equal nature, early research indicates that our DCI hits are closely linked to the cyclic nature of our bodies. "In short," she said, "if they [women] bubble, the event is more likely to be clustered in the first week of their cycle."

Marguerite St. Leger Dowse of the English Diving Disease Research Center (DDRC) seems to concur with her statements and agrees that it is not fair to make premature statements since it is hard to get a broad and equal statistical base. A DDRC study of over 2000 divers found "female divers to be less experienced and to retire from diving sooner." Since women have a shorter history of diving, there is a shortage in the statistical base.

But, the elements that interested me most in St. Leger-Dowse's study were not the physical observations, but some of the psychological issues. After giving retrospective questionnaires to women who were diving during their period, she compiled some interesting similarities. A majority of the respondents indicated that they felt physical differences during their period, yet only 12% said they were more conservative with diving plans during that time frame.

I believe that my encounter with DCS can be attributed to several different factors. Physical exertion before, during and after the dive, and repetitive extreme profiles contributed, in addition to the fact that I was just starting my period. Psychologically, I must also admit that I was swept up in the expedition fever of doing too much, too quickly with not enough support on hand. Although I am now subject to a greater statistical likelihood of getting bent again, I hope that I have learned enough from my experience to be a safer, smarter diver.

With a small statistical base and tables that have been tested primarily on men, women must listen to our hearts and be as conservative as possible. There are far more instances of bends in technical diving than DAN stats will ever be made aware of. In my circle of active explorers, I can name only a few, who have not experienced DCS. There is no reason to feel shame or embarrassment about the injury, and every reason to share the scars of your experiences whether they are physical or psychological. By sharing those experiences, you may help someone to get treatment faster.

Gear Issues

Recreational diving gear has gone through an amazing transformation since I started diving. The first equipment made specifically for women was just "small and pink," but now many buoyancy control devices and other types of equipment are sized and proportioned specifically for women. Unfortunately, there are still so few of us in the technical arena that we have to shop hard to find something that fits properly. If we want to be in the sport for decades to come, it means we have to take care of our backs, respect our limitations and be creative about how we get our equipment to the water's edge.

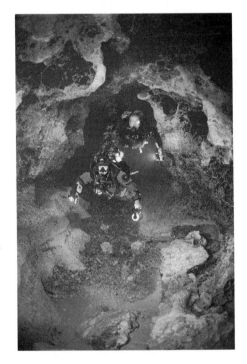

Cave Instructors Pam Wooten and Van Fleming at Ginnie Springs. Photo: Jill Heinerth

176

Some solutions I have found over the years include:

Sidemount Diving – I use this technique for exploration, but it is a great general diving solution if toting doubles is beyond your physical comfort. This way you can carry one tank at a time and get dressed in the water.

Dive Rite TransPac – This is perhaps the most versatile-fitting harness on the market and can be specifically fitted to a woman. It's not just off-the-shelf small, but you can interchange parts to make it all fit properly as long as the salesperson is knowledgeable about the options. Women have very short torsos compared to men, and an extra small harness back may accommodate your neck-to-waist measurement better.

Women's Backplate – Halcyon markets a short torso backplate specifically designed for women. It is worth checking to see if this fits you well.

Rebreathers – Although you still may be carrying multiple bailout bottles, a rebreather is a leaner package, and generally lighter to carry around. They require creativity and modification to achieve the best fit possible.

Drysuits – It's no secret that women get colder during diving. If you have gear that keeps you warm, you will dive a whole lot more. I wear a drysuit year-round in Florida. Latex seals are generally better for women than neoprene seals since our head-to-neck ratio is more dramatic than a man's more square profile. Getting a neoprene seal over your head, may take off a lot of skin, and still be loose around your neck. If you dive in an extremely cold environment, you can wear two hoods, dry gloves and extra thick underwear. Never wear cotton; always opt for high tech fibers such as Primaloft, Thinsulate or Capilene that will wick moisture and keep you warm even when wet. Have cozy, dry, after-dive clothing ready to wear including a hat. Santi Diving has released a "Ladies First" line of drysuits, undergarments and accessories. This entire line was developed specifically to meet the needs of women.

Heaters – If you dive in very cold water, Santi Diving has created a comprehensive line of heating devices including full suits, vests and even heated gloves.

Santi's heating system is very popular for women diving in cold water regions. Photo: Jill Heinerth

Immersion Diuresis

The most common question I get in cave parking lots is, "how do you manage the long dives?" Is there a solution for women and their inevitable need to pee? If you wear a wetsuit, let 'er rip. That is one hygiene factor you have to get over quickly if you want to dive a lot. Holding back is not just uncomfortable but also potentially harmful. If you dive in a drysuit, do not intentionally dehydrate prior to diving. Dehydration is present in most DCS cases and may contribute to hits. It's not pretty, but necessary to consider things such as adult diapers to get you through the long dives. Sometimes I have worn two diapers with bike shorts on top to try to keep them in place. Finally, there are two products that are available for women that want to use actual pee-valves as offboard dumps. The She-Pee and She-Wee-Go are both commercially available and supported. The She-Pee is a small silicone funnel that glues directly in place with medical adhesive. It requires shaving and has some potentially challenging hygiene and maintenance issues for women on expeditions. The She-Wee-Go is a rubber cup affixed to a G-string device and built into a pair of snug shorts. Shaving is also recommended but not imperative. Either product plugs into a basic men's pee valve, which must be installed into a drysuit. Both products take training and experimentation. Early attempts may result in leakage, frustration and possibly, unintended squeezes. In both cases, I have found that horizontal swimming positions while voiding work best. Slow and frequent urination seems less prone to leaks than high-velocity voiding. Although imperfect, these products are a large improvement over bulky diapers or dehydration.

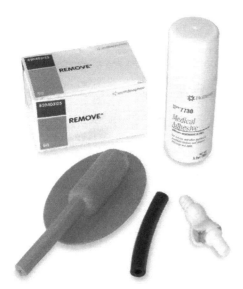

The She-P system. Photo provided by the manufacturer.

Gender Roles and Team Dynamics

Throughout my career in diving, I have run the gamut of different reactions from men about my activities. To this day, I am often still a lone woman in a sea of testosterone. In my early diving career, I felt like I had to work twice as hard to be respected. At other times, I felt like a novelty. While men were competing heavily for key positions on an expedition, I was sometimes applauded for just showing up. But the wisdom of experience has shown me that if I do my best, I will be treated equally and with great respect. On the exploration stage, I now understand that men often feel more pressured by competition with others, whereas women are competing only with themselves to do their best.

My best advice to women who are seeking opportunities in exploration is to have confidence, volunteer and speak up when you desire an opportunity. Seek other women as mentors, who can ease the way and answer questions. It is still such a small community that most of us also crave the participation and camaraderie of diving with other women.

Women Divers Hall of Fame

In 2000, the Women Divers Hall of Fame (WDHOF) was established to celebrate the accomplishments of women in diving. The organization offers numerous scholarships and training grants each year, and many of the individual members support women in the community through mentoring and internships. The website, www.wdhof.org details such opportunities.

Cave Photography

Even before you take the first shot, there are many important things to consider when taking photographs in caves. Your skills should be excellent. Safety is critical and you should assign your model to be responsible as a safety officer. Creative pursuits are a task load and take your mind away from important things such as monitoring bottom time and air supply. Cave conservation is also far more important than the shot. Your buoyancy and awareness must be excellent.

Use a Model

Always use a model to give the cave a sense of scale and wonder. The model will double as your safety officer, and their skills must be as good as yours to protect the cave and complete a safe and successful shoot.

Think about Light

The cavern zone is one the prettiest places to shoot. Learn to see and appreciate available light, and learn how to control it. Take advantage of ambient light and then supplement with justified light (light that appears to come from a diver's source).

Know the Capabilities of Your Gear

It takes a significant investment to shoot anything more than a simple head-shot on a black background. Start slowly, in the cavern zone, to learn about the capabilities of your equipment. Shooting in an automatic mode will rarely result in a balanced exposure, and strobes set to TTL will not be the best answer for any scenario. Most stunning cave photos have utilized multiple slave strobes with carefully chosen manual exposures. GoPro cameras are convenient but need substantial light to bring a cave photo to life.

Murphy's Law of Strobes

Underwater strobes can be finicky, especially slave strobes. Test them on the surface and test again when you first enter the water. Then assume that you may only have limited success with them in the cave! Slave strobes will accidentally fire if triggered by the quick motion of a cave light. They sometimes trigger from impact. You may want to arrive at your shooting location before powering them up, then set them on the most sensitive setting so they only fire when triggered by the master strobe. Slave batteries should be changed regularly to ensure that they fire when desired. Luckily many newer strobes fuel the slave sensor with the main, rechargeable batteries, lessening the likelihood of failure.

You might consider using continuous light as opposed to a strobe. The light will need to be of significant power with a wide beam. Light & Motion Sola series video lights are a good example, such as the Sola 3000. Lights upwards to 4000 to 8000 lumens may be needed to fill larger spaces in the cave with light.

Lenses

Wide-angle lenses are a favorite among cave shooters to adequately capture the spacious environment while getting the photographer close to the diver. This allows for shooting in much lower visibility conditions than other lenses. If you are close to your subject, you won't need, as much light to illuminate the scene and the colors will be richer.

Modern Cameras

Most photographers shoot digitally these days, but there are a few challenges with this type of camera. It may be hard to focus in complete blackness, when you are set to auto focus. You may need to bring in a diffused wide beam light to help illuminate the scene and assist with focus. The viewfinder can appear deceptively bright in complete darkness so you should learn to shoot using histograms as feedback, rather than the image in the viewfinder. Choose to shoot in RAW format if available. Each pixel will net over 4000 levels of brightness, as opposed to a JPG file that will only give you 256 levels of brightness per pixel. Although they will look identical on your computer screen (which only displays 256 levels of brightness) the adjustability of the image is far greater in programs such as Lightroom or Photoshop.

Advanced Lighting - In the Cavern

Get shallow and look at ambient light angles. Use 1/125th of a second or faster to freeze beams of light. Supplement the ambient light with a well-balanced and subtle quarter-power fill flash. Add to that, with a wide beamed, hand-held light that gently fills a diver's mask, illuminating their eyes.

Single Slave Photography

Slave strobes are flashes that are triggered by a primary strobe that is mounted to the camera. Slave sensors are either built in to the strobe head or are connected with a cable from the main strobe body. The strobe can be mounted on a diver's body and directed to flash behind them, illuminating the cave. In this case, a remote sensor pointing towards the camera will be needed for effective triggering. Slave strobes can also be placed in the cave behind formations or hung from the ceiling to cast a light from above.

Backlighting with Slave Strobes

Backlighting can be achieved when the diver in the rear hides the strobe from the camera but points the slave sensor and strobe in the direction of the lens. Hiding the strobe directly behind the lead diver will surround them with a glowing backlight. The sensor eye needs to be visible by the master strobe to fire.

Backlight provided by a slave strobe places on a ledge behind the diver.
Photo: Jill Heinerth

Multiple Slave Strobes

The more strobes you add to a shot, the greater the challenge. Using multiple, fixed, slave strobes will take a long time to set up and execute a shot. It is a balance of hiding units in the right locations while ensuring that the slave sensor eyes are able to read the light from the primary strobe or another slave in the cave. Weights or rigging may be needed to secure the strobes in the right location and direction.

If your team intends to swim with multiple slave strobes, then a rehearsal on land is warranted. Direct each swimmer about their role as someone providing backlight or front lighting. Fixed lighting uses high-powered video lights such as Light & Motion's Sola series can be used in place of strobes with a high quality camera.

Caves can be brightly lit by multiple slave strobes: Photo: Jill Heinerth

Painting with Strobes

Painting techniques can be very effective if the camera can be set on a tripod. Set the camera on "B" so the shutter stays open until you depress it again, or you can set a long time exposure of a minute or two. One strobe may be manually fired in many different locations or the cave can be painted with rapid strokes of a wide beam light. A camera operator swimming in front of the lens to manipulate strobes must shield any light from the camera or he will appear in the photo in whole or in ghost form. The photographer can hold their hand in front of the lens while divers move from place to place to facilitate the next flash of a strobe.

A light painting of Little River cave basin. Photo: Jill Heinerth

Shootings with Histograms

When I first transitioned to digital photography, I was disappointed that photos shot underwater in the cave looked excellent on the screen, but were underexposed, when downloaded to my computer. The LCD screen can lure you into thinking you have a great shot, especially when viewed in low-light conditions. With a good understanding of a feature called histograms, you will get a much higher percentage of well-exposed photographs.

The histogram is a metering function of the camera, which is viewed on the LCD screen, after the image is shot. As a matter of practice, the LCD photo image should only be used to evaluate composition, whereas the histogram should be used to critique exposure.

Traditional photographic film only provides an acceptable exposure in the range of a few f-stops. Today's digital camera sensors can record a larger range of acceptable light, considered to be around five or six f-stops. Some underwater cameras may offer a wide range of 10 or 12 f-stops in a shot. A histogram display gives you a visual representation of what has been shot and what can be adjusted.

How to Read Histograms

A histogram is a bar graph that shows you 256 brightness levels for your image from pure black on the left to pure white on the right. It also allows you to see the distribution of tones in an image. The taller the peak of a bar on the graph, the more of that particular color, you will see in the photo. The more pixels on the right, the brighter the image. The more pixels on the left, the darker the image. An underexposed photo will show all the pixels stacked on the left and an overexposed photo will show all the pixels piled on the right. A flat looking photo will contain a mountain of pixels bunched in the middle. A contrasty photo will have tall peaks on each end of the histogram.

When reviewing a histogram, concentrate mainly on the far left and far right. If bars fill up the left of the screen and peak at the top, then critical information has been lost. You cannot lighten the darkest area to recover detail if the histogram peaks on the left. The converse is true on the right side. If the bars fill up the right side and peak at the top, then there are areas of complete whiteness without any detail remaining. When the right or left side of the histogram is filled to the top of the graph, we call this "clipping."

Well-distributed peaks and valleys allow for a lot of adjustment in image editing programs, although a histogram does not need to cover an entire window. An underwater cave image should not clip on the left, but most of the data will still fill the left side of the bar graph since this dark blue environment does not contain all the colors of the spectrum.

Using Histograms to Make Adjustments

Many digital cameras offer several viewing options on the LCD screen. The full frame image is a good tool for composition and a reasonable judge for serious focusing errors. The "highlight" screen, available on some cameras, will flicker the area where white has been

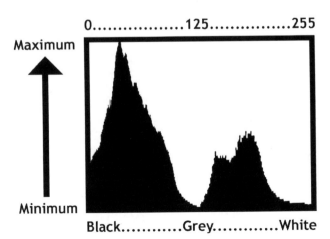

0..................125................255

Maximum

Minimum

Black...........Grey............White

clipped from the image. The human eye is not very forgiving to an image with blown-out white areas or highlights, but understands better, an image with dark, clipped shadow areas. We call dark photos artistic and moody but clipped highlights are considered overexposed mistakes. Refer to the histogram screen after you shoot an image and quickly scan it for clipping on either end. Exposure and composition adjustments can then be made to improve the next shot.

Once you have mastered using histograms, you can use them to create a very unique "look" for your photos and return from every dive with well-exposed shots that can be improved in image-editing programs.

The histogram on the left shows an over exposed shot and the diagram on the right shows an under exposed photo. Diagrams: Jill Heinerth

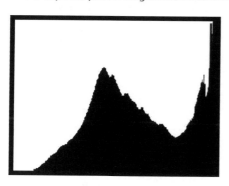 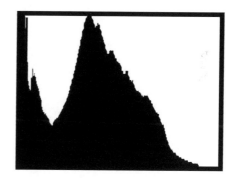

Travel Issues

When traveling with cave diving gear, rebreather, or photographic equipment, make a formal equipment list with the following information: quantity of items, description of item, country of origin (manufacturer), value of item, and case/bag number that the gear is packed in. Add a line item called "personal diving equipment" and give it a high value (this will cover all the things you forgot to list!)

Customs

If you are traveling with an amount of gear exceeding normal limits, or if you are on a commercial project, register all of your gear with customs at your local international airport, port or Customs and Border Control Office and get at least two stamped documents from them. If you are working for a company or educational institution, get a letter of intent from them that you can use at

185

your destination to confirm the work you are doing. If it is your own company, put a letter on your own letterhead. If you are simply traveling for vacation, keep it simple and do not offer Custom's agents anything that you are not asked for first.

Work Visas

If you are working for hire or a member of a scientific expedition, you may need a formal work visa from the country you are visiting. The host country will also want a letter that indicates that all of your excessive gear will return to your home country after your job is completed. Work visas are usually obtained in the US and Canada at the Consular office for the country that you are visiting, and they usually require application in person or temporary surrender of your passport.

Go to the Ministry of Tourism for the host country, and ask for their assistance for travel, logistics, complimentary accommodations, etc. Some national airlines may help you out if you publish an article that will benefit tourism.

Packing

Spend good money getting good luggage. With current TSA scrutiny, your gear bags/cases may be opened several times in your absence. Place a gear list on the inside lid of the case or bag with a large heading, such as, "diving and photographic gear – safe for airline transport." Do not wrap fragile items in clothing. An inspector may pick up a t-shirt and send your delicate lens or primary light crashing to the pavement. Remove the main O-ring from your camera housing to avoid over-pressurization damage. Do the same for sealed rebreather canisters and primary lights. Mark the inside and outside of the case "fragile."

If possible, leave a rebreather assembled, but remove tank valves completely from any cylinders. Tape over the end of the tank with clear packing tape and put masking tape over anything that says "oxygen." On the inside of a rebreather case, place a note with a photo of yourself wearing the rebreather with a big smile on your face. The note should briefly explain that your equipment is life support and is very fragile. It should be boldly addressed "Dear TSA..." Put your cell phone number on the note and encourage the TSA officer to contact you if they have questions. Put your flight number and destination on the note too. If your bag or case is secured with zip ties or tape, place additional zip ties and tape inside with instructions to replace anything that has been removed.

Ensure your primary lights are disabled during travel so there is no way they can accidentally turn on and start a fire. Any extra batteries must be carried in carryon baggage now and may not be checked. If you are traveling with a scooter, check to ensure that the battery meets the size limits for passenger aircraft. Most lithium scooter batteries will need to be sent ahead as cargo.

Baggage Restrictions

If you carry more than a regular allotment of luggage you should tell the airline in advance, when you buy your ticket. Many airlines have moratoriums on extra baggage. That means no exceptions for carrying extra baggage. Most airlines allow two fifty-pound bags, in addition to one carry on, of forty pounds, and a computer or purse on international flights. Small planes such as the ones you take between Caribbean or South Pacific islands have even more stringent limitations. Some international airports, such as Britain's Heathrow, limit clients to one carry on bag. Sometimes it is cheaper to go overweight than to add an extra bag, so carefully research baggage limits before you travel. They change often and should be reviewed immediately before travel.

It is wise to get a "notation in your ticket booking file" so that when the ticketing agent pulls up your reservation, a note appears on their screen indicating that you are cleared for extra baggage. Some airlines even allow you to pay for extra baggage online in advance, and they may also offer a discount for the advanced notification, however, they may only guarantee delivery of a limited number of bags. Finally, double-check with the airlines to confirm that you can pack your tools, since they are almost never allowable in carry on limits.

Insurance

If you can't afford to replace your gear, consider insurance on your equipment. Some household insurance will cover minimal quantities of gear if they are itemized on the homeowner's policy. Other equipment insurance programs are now available through DAN and other agency partnerships.

Other Considerations for Travel

Check with your destination prior to travel about other necessities that may be needed. Do they have DIN valves or will you need regulator adapters? Are the DIN valves 300 bar? If so, a 200 bar DIN regulator will not fit. Do you need power converters? Do you need cheaters (two-pronged adapters for countries without grounding sockets, such as Mexico). Are there plentiful outlets or should you bring a power bar so you can easily recharge your lights? Do you need wing nuts? Do you need wrenches to move bands to fit the 11-inch spacing on your backplate? What will you do if the tank bolts are too short on your set of rental doubles? Will you need a certification card? Which type? Will you need proof of oxygen training? If traveling overseas, does the destination require European M25 oxygen fittings? Will you need a different oxygen regulator? Will you need a fill block to fill your DIN tank? If you are doing your own fills, will you need any different transfer whips and fittings? Do you need a special permit to rent T-cylinders from the gas company? Can you get HP oxygen for your rebreather? What type of sorb is available?

These questions may seem like minor issues, but I seen expeditions delayed for such simple and preventable issues. Things that are easy to obtain at home may be very difficult and expensive to get in foreign countries. Plan ahead.

The author stands by the gear needed for a small National Geographic shoot in Andros, Bahamas. This small mountain of gear did not even include the tanks for the team of six divers.

GLOSSARY OF CAVE & REBREATHER TERMS

CHAPTER 11

Glossary of Cave Diving and Rebreather Terminology--

A

Absolute pressure – The total pressure imposed by the depth of water plus the atmospheric pressure at the surface.

Absorbent pads – Absorbent material placed in breathing loop; used to soak up moisture caused by condensation and metabolism.

Accumulator – A small chamber that provides a collection vessel to ensure proper gas flow of oxygen to a solenoid valve.

Active-addition – A rebreather gas-addition system that actively injects gas into the breathing loop (such as a constant-mass flow valve in certain kinds of semiclosed rebreathers).

Atmospheres absolute (ata) – The absolute pressure as measured in atmospheres.

Atmosphere (atm) – A unit of pressure equivalent to the mean pressure exerted by the Earth's atmosphere at sea level, or by 33 fsw, or by 10 msw (equal to 1.0 bar or 14.7 psi).

Automatic diluent valve (ADV) – A mechanically activated valve that adds diluent gas when increasing pressure associated with descent or lowered volume triggers the device.

Axial scrubber – A type of CO_2 absorbent canister design. In this design, the gas flows through the canister in a linear fashion from one end of the canister to the other.

Azimuth – Compass bearing.

B

Backplate – A plate made of stainless steel, aluminum or acrylonitrile butadiene styrene (ABS) plastic, which attaches to a rebreather and allows for the use of a webbed or soft harness system.

Bailout – A failure requiring a dive to be terminated, usually using open-circuit gas.

Bailout gas – Tanks carried by the diver to allow for escape from a serious situation, often conducted with open-circuit technique.

Bailout valve (BOV) – An open-circuit regulator built into the mouthpiece assembly that allows a diver to switch from closed-circuit mode to open-circuit without removing the mouthpiece from their mouth. When the loop is closed, the BOV activates, supplying open-circuit gas directly from the onboard diluent tank (in a closed-circuit rebreather) or supply gas cylinder (in a semiclosed-circuit rebreather).

Bar – A unit measure of pressure, roughly equivalent to 1 atm.

Barotrauma – A pressure related injury.

Biospeleology – the study of the unique biology of caves.

Bottom-out (counterlung) – A term used to refer to the situation when a re-breather counterlung becomes completely collapsed after a full inhalation.

Boom scenario – An explosion or implosion of a hose or other component usually resulting in rapid gas loss or catastrophic loop failure.

Boyle's Law – The volume occupied by a given number of gas molecules is inversely proportional the pressure of the gas.

Breakdown – refers to a room containing a boulder pile or slope of debris, which likely crumbled from the ceiling at one time in its development.

Breakthrough – the point at which a scrubber allows CO_2 to bypass the scrubbing process to be re-inspired. The fraction of inspired CO_2 normally rises extremely quickly once breakthrough is reached.

Breathing hose – Large bore hoses in a rebreather breathing loop, through which the breathing gas travels.

Breathing loop – The portion of a rebreather through which gas circulates, usually consisting of a mouthpiece, breathing hose(s), counterlungs, non-return valves and a CO_2 absorbent canister.

Buddy lights – Warning lights that indicate system status including life-threatening oxygen levels; usually monitored by the buddy diver.

Buoyancy control device (BCD) – An inflatable bladder which allows a diver to precisely adjust buoyancy.

C

Calibration gas – A gas of a known composition used to calibrate gas sensors, particularly PO_2 and PCO_2 sensors.

Caletta – A term used in Mexico that refers to the location where a freshwater spring empties into a coastal lagoon.

Calibration gas – A gas of a known composition used to calibrate gas sensors, particularly PO_2 and PCO_2 sensors.

Chain of custody – Refers to the chronological documentation that captures the seizure, custody, control, transfer, analysis, and disposition of physical or electronic evidence, typically for legal purposes.

Channeling (of scrubber canister) – Condition in which improper packing or excessive settling forms channels that allow some CO_2 to pass through the scrubber without being absorbed.

Check valve – A one-way, non-return valve that directs gas to move in only one direction through the breathing loop.

Chemosynthesis – The biological conversion of nutrients into organic matter using the oxidation of inorganic molecules as a source of energy, rather than sunlight, as in photosynthesis.

Circuit dive – a cave dive that takes a circular route through a cave, but begins and ends in the same entrance.

Closed-circuit rebreather (CCR) – A type of rebreather that usually includes some form of oxygen control system and generally only vents gas upon ascent.

CO_2 absorbent – A material that chemically binds with CO_2 molecules (Sodasorb, Drägersorb,® lithium hydroxide, Sofnolime,® Micropore ExtendAir, etc.).

CO_2 absorbent canister – A canister in the breathing loop containing CO_2 absorbent.

Condensation – Water that forms when water vapor cools and forms liquid droplets. In a rebreather, heat conduction through the breathing hoses and other components of the breathing loop lead to condensation. This process may be exacerbated by materials with greater heat conductivity and lessened with insulation of the breathing loop components.

Conduction (thermal) – Heat flow between objects in physical contact; the inverse of insulation.

Constant mass flow valve – A type of valve that allows a constant mass of gas molecules to flow at a fixed rate.

Constant volume flow – a type of valve that delivers a constant volume, independent of ambient pressure, thus a flexible number of gas molecules.

Convection (thermal) – Heat flow through circulating currents in liquid or gas environment.

Counterlung – A collapsible bag connected to a rebreather breathing loop, which expands as a diver exhales and collapses as a diver inhales.

Cubic feet (ft³) – A unit measure of volume, defined as the space occupied by a cube one foot on each side; 1 ft³ = 28.3 L.

Current limited (oxygen sensor) – a condition in which a change in the load applied to a sensor is not met with a change in the current supplied by the sensor.

D

Dalton's law (of partial pressures) – States that the total pressure exerted by the mixture of gases is equal to the sum of the partial pressures of individual gases.

dcCCR – Diver-controlled closed-circuit rebreather. A manually operated rebreather which requires the diver to monitor oxygen levels and manually inject oxygen as needed to maintain an appropriate setpoint. Also known as a manual CCR (mCCR).

Decompression dive – Any dive that requires staged stops during ascent (determined by the decompression algorithm used).

Decompression model/algorithm – Mathematical algorithm used to compute decompression procedures. A variety of computational models and derivatives are available in tabular or dive computer form.

Decompression illness (DCI) – Injury that includes arterial gas embolism (AGE) and decompression sickness (DCS).

Decompression sickness (DCS) – Injury seen especially in divers, caused by the formation of inert gas bubbles in the blood and tissues following a sudden drop in the surrounding pressure, as when ascending rapidly from a dive, and characterized by severe pains in the joints, skin irritation, paralysis, and other symptoms.

Demand regulator – A valve that delivers gas from a pressurized source at or near ambient atmospheric pressure when the diver inhales.

Diffusion – The process in which molecules move from a region of high concentration to a region of low concentration.

Diluent – A cylinder in a closed-circuit rebreather that contains a supply of gas which is used to make up the substantial volume within the breathing loop; a mixture capable of diluting pure oxygen.

Diluent purge valve/diluent addition valve – A manual valve used to add diluent gas to a breathing loop, usually through the counterlung or a gas block assembly.

Display integrated vibrating alarm (DIVA) – A light-emitting diode (LED) heads-up display module mounted close to the diver's mask, offering information about various states of the rebreather such as PO_2; this style includes a vibrating warning alarm when oxygen levels are unsafe.

Dissolution cave – The longest and most complex type of cave. They occur where carbonate, sedimentary rocks, such as limestone or dolomite, have been dissolved by natural forces over time.

Downstream – a relative direction with respect to the flow of gas through the breathing loop of a rebreather; the direction of travel of the diver's exhaled gas.

Or

Swimming with the direction of water flow.

Downstream check-valve – A one-way, non-return valve that directs exhaled gas to flow in one direction only, for a rebreather. This would typically be the mushroom-type valves that prevent subsequent re-inhalation of used gas and directs exhaled gas towards the CO_2 scrubber canister.

Dynamic setpoint – Also referred to as a floating setpoint, it is a setpoint that changes to optimize gas use, no stop time and other consumables and dive variables. The floating setpoint can be determined by an electronic system or modified manually by a diver using a mCCR.

E

Equivalent air depth (EAD) – A formula used to help approximate the decompression requirements of nitrox. The depth is expressed relative to the partial pressure of nitrogen in a normal breathing air.

eCCR – An electronically controlled closed-circuit rebreather in which an electronics package is used to monitor oxygen levels, add oxygen as needed and warn the diver of developing problems through a series of audible, visual and/or tactile alarm systems.

Elastic load – A load on the respiratory muscles originating from the rebreather and/or diving suit. Materials in the suit and rebreathing bag may restrict breathing. As the diver breathes, the volume of rebreathing bag(s) changes making the depth of the bag(s) change. This depth change means a change in pressure. Since the pressure change varies with bag volume it is, by definition, an elastic load.

Electronically-monitored mSCR – A mechanical SCR with electronic monitoring. Electronics are used to inform the diver of PO_2 as well as provide warnings and status updates, however the gas control is manually controlled by the diver.

Endurance (of scrubber) – the time for which a CO_2 scrubber operates effectively. The duration varies with individual size, work rate, scrubbing material, depth, and ambient temperature.

Equivalent narcotic depth (END) – A formula used as a way of estimating the narcotic effect of a breathing mixture such as heliox or trimix.

eSCR – An electronic semiclosed-circuit rebreather where an electronics package monitors the PO_2 and adds gas to maintain a floating setpoint that optimizes gas use and compensates for changing levels of diver exertion.

Enriched air nitrox (EAN) – A gas mixture consisting of nitrogen and oxygen; with more than 21% oxygen.

Evaporation (thermal) – The heat energy expended to convert liquid water to gaseous state. Evaporative heat loss results from humidifying inspired gases and the evaporation of sweat on the skin.

Exhalation counterlung – The counterlung downstream of the diver's mouthpiece.

F

Failure mode, effect, and criticality analysis (FMECA) – Summarizes the study of all components that could fail, and identifies the type of failure, the probability, and severity as well as possible causes of the failure and mitigation and emergency procedures.

ffw – Water depth as measured in feet of freshwater.

Floating setpoint (dynamic setpoint) – a setpoint that changes to optimize gas use, no stop time and other consumables and dive variables. The floating setpoint can be determined by an electronic system or modified manually by a diver using a mCCR.

Flowing sink – see Karst window.

Flush (as in flushing the loop) – Replacing the gas within the breathing loop by injecting gas and venting bubbles around the edge of the mouthpiece or through a vent valve.

FHe – The fraction of helium in a gas mixture.

FN$_2$ – The fraction of nitrogen in a gas mixture.

FO$_2$ – The fraction of oxygen in a gas mixture.

Fraction of gas – The percent of a particular gas in a gas mix.

Fraction of inspired gas – The fraction of gas actually inspired by the diver.

Fraction of inspired oxygen (F$_i$O$_2$) – The fraction of oxygen inspired by the diver. In SCR operation, this figure is calculated using a formula that takes into account the diver's workload.

fsw – Water depth as measured in feet of seawater.

Full-face mask – Mask system that encompasses the entire face, in contrast with a typical regulator held in the mouth alone.

G

Gap – a space between two ends of a guideline.

Galvanic fuel cell sensor – an electrochemical transducer that generates a current signal output that is both proportional and linear to the partial pressure of oxygen in the sample gas. Oxygen diffuses through a sensing membrane and reaches the cathode where it is reduced by electrons furnished by simultaneous oxidation of the anode.

Gas narcosis – A form of mental incapacity experienced by people while breathing an elevated partial pressure of a gas.

Gradient factor – a mathematical model applied to permit a diver to select the degree of conservatism or risk of their decompression profile.

H

Halocline – water of differing salinity, which becomes stratified in layers, disturbing normal vision.

Harness – The straps and/or soft pack that secures the rebreather to the diver.

Head Pool – The basin of water at the entrance of a cave or spring; also known as a spring vent, spring basin, headspring or simply basin.

Heads-up display (HUD) – A light-emitting diode (LED) display module mounted close to the diver's mask offering information about various conditions within rebreathers, such as PO$_2$.

Heat exchange – Divers experience four primary avenues of heat exchange in the diving environment - radiation, conduction, evaporation and convection.

Helictite – a complex speleothem that has been subjected to wind during its formative stages.

Heliox – A binary gas mixture consisting of helium and oxygen.

Helium (He) – An inert gas used as a component of breathing gas mixtures for deep dives because of its very low density and lack of narcotic potency.

Henry's law – The amount of gas that will dissolve in a liquid is proportional to the partial pressure of the gas over the liquid.

Histo – caver slang describing a disease caused form exposure to histoplasmosa capsulatum.

Histoplasma capsulatum – a fungus that grows in soil and material contaminated with bird or bat droppings; often found in caves.

Hydrogen sulfide – the chemical compound with the formula H_2S. Found as a layer in caves where decomposition is present.

Hydrophobic membrane – A special membrane that allows gas to flow through it, but serves as a barrier to water.

Hydrostatic imbalance – See static lung load.

Hyperbaric chamber – A rigid pressure vessel used in hyperbaric medicine. Such chambers can be run at absolute pressures up to six atmospheres (more for some research chambers) and may be used to treat divers suffering from decompression illness.

Hyperbaric medicine – Also known as hyperbaric oxygen therapy, is the medical use of oxygen at a higher than atmospheric pressure.

Hypercapnia/Hypercarbia – Elevated levels of CO_2 in the body due to inadequate breathing, generally induced by elevated respiratory loads and/or inspired CO_2. The level of CO_2 maintained varies from person to person (e.g., CO_2 retainers maintain relatively high levels). Effects of hypercapnia may include shortness of breath, headaches, migraines, confusion, impaired judgment, augmented narcosis, panic attacks, and loss of consciousness. Dangerous levels can be reached while the diver remains unaware. Recovery may take many minutes under optimal conditions.

Hyperoxia – A concentration of oxygen in the breathing mixture that is not tolerated by the human body, generally occurring when the inspired PO_2 rises above about 1.6 ata. Symptoms include visual and auditory disturbances, nausea, irritability, twitching, and dizziness; hyperoxia may result in convulsions and drowning without warning.

Hyperoxic linearity – The condition that a PO_2 sensor is linear at partial pressures of oxygen above the highest calibration point.

Hypothermia – Condition of low body temperature, defined by a core temperature falling below 35ºC (95ºF), substantially below the normal core temperature range of 36.5-37.5ºC (97.7-99.5ºF). Reaching a state of frank hypothermia is very unlikely in normal operational diving.

Hypoxia – A concentration of oxygen in the breathing mixture that is insufficient to support human life, generally occurring when inspired PO_2 drops below 0.16 ata.

I

Inhalation counterlung – The counterlung upstream from the diver's mouth-piece block.

Insulation (thermal) – The resistance in heat flow between objects in physical contact; the inverse of conduction. The standard unit of insulation is the 'clo,' with 1.0 clo (1 clo = $0.18°C·m^2·h·kcal^{-1}$ = $0.155°C·m^2·W^{-1}$ = 5.55 kcal·$m^2·h^{-1}$).

Integrated open-circuit regulator – A second-stage, open-circuit regulator, which is built-in to a mouthpiece block; also known as a bailout valve (BOV).

J

Jump – a situation where a diver leaves the main guideline and bridges over to a side passage, creating a temporary "T" in the line with their reel.

K

Karst – A landscape shaped by the dissolution of a layer or layers of soluble carbonate rock such as limestone or dolomite.

Karst window – Also flowing sink. A term referring to a spring/siphon complex. Upstream and downstream flow is both present in a single pool.

L

Layering (thermal protection) – Base layer (hydrophobic) to wick water away from the skin and reduce conductive heat flow; mid-layer with high insulation value to reduce conductive heat flow; shell layer barrier to reduce convective heat flow.

Liquid crystal display (LCD) – an energy efficient display that relies on the light modulating properties of liquid crystals.

Light-emitting diode (LED) – a small, low power light source used for warning lights on rebreathers.

Line trap – Occurs when a carelessly placed line falls out of position and into a space through which a diver may not fit.

Lithium hydroxide (LiOH) – A type of CO_2 absorbent material.

Loop vent valve – The adjustable overpressure-relief valve attached to the bottom of the exhalation counterlung, which allows excess gas and accumulated water in the breathing loop to be vented. Also known as an OPV.

M

M-Value – Describes the "maximum" value that a tissue compartment can tolerate, without exhibiting signs of over-pressurization or supersaturation.

Manual bypass valve – A valve on a rebreather that allows the diver to manually inject gas into the breathing loop.

Manual diluent addition valve – The valve on a rebreather that allows diluent gas to be manually injected into the breathing loop.

Manual oxygen addition valve – The valve on a rebreather that allows oxygen to be manually injected into the breathing loop.

Maximum operating depth (MOD) - The maximum operating depth of a breathing gas before reaching a predetermined PO_2, usually 1.4 ata or higher. This depth is determined to safeguard the diver from oxygen toxicity.

mCCR – A manually operated closed-circuit rebreather which requires the diver to monitor oxygen levels and manually inject oxygen as needed to maintain an appropriate setpoint. Also known as dcCCR or diver-controlled CCR.

Metabolism – The physiological process where nutrients are broken down to provide energy. This process involves the consumption of oxygen and the production of CO_2.

mfw – Water depth as measures in meters of freshwater.

Mixed-gas rebreather – A rebreather that contains a gas mixture other than pure oxygen in the breathing loop.

Mouthpiece (of CCR) – The portion of a rebreather breathing loop through which the diver breathes. This usually includes a way to prevent water from entering the breathing loop and sometimes includes an integrated open-circuit regulator (BOV).

msw – Water depth as measured in meters of seawater.

N

Narcosis – A form of mental incapacity experienced by people while breathing an elevated partial pressure of a gas such as nitrogen or CO_2.

Near eye rebreather display (NERD) – A heads-up display that duplicates the wrist unit or primary controller.

Nitrox – See enriched air nitrox.

No-decompression dive – Any dive that allows a diver to ascend directly to the surface, without the need for staged decompression stops. Also referred to as a no-stop dive.

Normoxic – A mixture of gas containing 0.21 ata oxygen.

Notified body – Agent that acts as the certifying authority and verifies that equipment testing was conducted properly in compliance with all applicable requirements.

O

Offboard diluent – A diluent gas tank that is clipped externally to a rebreather.

Offboard oxygen – An oxygen tank that is clipped externally to a rebreather.

Offset sink – A sinkhole which still retains base level flow from either an upstream or downstream direction.

Organic light-emitting diode (OLED) - A display type that does not use a back-light and is able to display rich blacks that offer greater contrast in low light applications such as diving.

Onboard diluent – A diluent tank that is integrally mounted on a rebreather.

Onboard diluent regulator – A first-stage regulator which attaches to the onboard diluent tank of a rebreather.

Onboard oxygen – An oxygen tank that is integrally mounted on a rebreather.

Onboard oxygen regulator – A first-stage regulator which attaches to the onboard oxygen tank.

Overpressure relief valve (OPV) – the adjustable valve attached to the bottom of the exhalation counterlung, which allows excess gas and accumulated water in the breathing loop to be vented; also known as a loop vent valve.

Open-circuit scuba (OC) – Self-contained underwater breathing apparatus where the inhaled breathing gas is supplied from a high-pressure cylinder to the diver via a two-stage pressure reduction demand regulator, and the exhaled gas is vented into the surrounding water and discarded in the form of bubbles.

Optode – an optical sensor device that measures a specific substance usually with the aid of a chemical transducer.

Oxygen consumption (VO$_2$) – a measure of the work intensity. Resting VO$_2$ is usually assumed to be 3.5 mL·kg^{-1}·min^{-1} (1 metabolic equivalent [MET]). Aerobic capacity (VO$_{2max}$) can be described as multiples of 1.0 MET. Recommendations for minimum VO$_{2max}$ to be maintained by divers range from a low of >6.0 MET to >13 MET.

Oxygen (O$_2$) control system – The components of a rebreather which manage the concentration of oxygen in the breathing loop. The system usually includes sensors, electronics and a solenoid valve that injects oxygen.

Oxygen rebreather – A type of closed-circuit rebreather that incorporates only oxygen as a gas supply. The earliest form of closed-circuit rebreather, designed for covert military operations, submarine escape and mine rescue operations.

Oxygen (O$_2$) sensor – Any sensor that produces a signal related to O$_2$ pressure or concentration. In diving, the most common type is a galvanic cell that generates an electrical voltage that is proportional in strength to the partial pressure of oxygen exposed to the sensor.

Oxygen toxicity – Symptoms experienced by individuals suffering exposures to oxygen that are above normal ranges tolerated by human physiology. See pulmonary oxygen toxicity and central nervous system oxygen toxicity.

P

Partial pressure – The portion of the total gas pressure exerted by a single constituent of a gas mixture calculated by multiplying the fraction of the gas by the absolute pressure of the gas.

Passive addition – Gas addition systems utilized by some semiclosed-circuit rebreathers to passively inject gas into the breathing loop; usually achieved by a mechanical valve that opens in response to a collapsed bellow or drop in breathing loop gas pressure.

PN_2 – The partial pressure of nitrogen in a gas mixture, usually referring specifically to the breathing gas mixture inhaled by a diver.

PCO_2 – The partial pressure of carbon dioxide in a gas mixture, usually referring specifically to the breathing gas mixture inhaled by a diver.

Phreatic – refers to submerged cave conduits that were formed and/or enlarged below the water table.

PO_2 – The partial pressure of oxygen in a gas mixture, usually referring specifically to the breathing gas mixture inhaled by a diver.

PO_2 setpoint – The PO_2 set by the diver, used to determine when a solenoid valve injects oxygen into the breathing loop.

Pozo – see sinkhole.

psi – Unit of pressure measured in pound per square inch (1 psi = 55 mm Hg = 6.9 kPa).

Pulmonary oxygen toxicity – Pulmonary irritation typically caused by prolonged exposure to breathing mixtures with oxygen partial pressures in excess of 0.5 ata. This form of oxygen toxicity primarily affects the lungs and causes pain on deep inhalation as well as other symptoms.

S

Safety stops – Stops carried out during ascent not required by the decompression model being followed for the dive.

Scrubber – See CO_2 absorbent.

Semiclosed-circuit rebreather (SCR) – A type of rebreather that injects a mixture of nitrox or mixed gas into a breathing loop to replace that which is used by the diver for metabolism; excess gas is periodically vented into the surrounding water in the form of bubbles.

Sensor validation – Methods to confirm the appropriate function of sensors, typically oxygen sensors.

Setpoint – See PO_2 setpoint.

Shoulder port – The plastic shoulder connectors in a breathing loop which connect the breathing hoses to the counterlungs, sometimes serving as water traps to divert condensation and leaked water into the counterlungs and down to the overpressure relief valve (OPV).

Sinkhole – A collapse caused gradually or suddenly, by dissolution from percolating water. Often the shape of an hourglass, containing a debris mound, known as a talus cone, at the bottom. Also blue hole, cenote, pozo.

Siphon – A cave opening into which water flows downstream. Also known as ponors, go-away holes, sucks, sinks, syphons, swallets and estavelles. Also insurgence.

Skip breathing - The practice of inhaling, holding the breath and then exhaling slowly in order to attempt to extend the time underwater by using less air. This practice can lead to buildup of CO_2 (hypercapnia).

Sodalime – A general term referring to a chemical agent that reacts and bonds with CO_2 and is commonly used in the scrubbers of rebreathers.

Solenoid valve – A valve that opens when electricity is applied to an electromagnetic solenoid coil; usually the type of valve used to inject oxygen into the breathing loop of a closed-circuit rebreather.

Solid-state sensor – a sensor with no mobile parts that detects or measures a physical property.

Speleogenesis – The development or formation of caves. It often deals with the development of caves through dissolution of limestone, caused by the presence of water with carbon dioxide dissolved within it, producing carbonic acid.

Speleothems – Delicate carbonate formations on the ceilings and floors of caves, which were formed from dripping water. Columns, stalactites, stalagmites, helictites, rim pools, shields and pearls are types of speleothems.

Spring - a cave opening or vent from which water is erupting. Also resurgence.

Spring run - the small stream leading from the spring entrance to another water body such as a river.

Stack – Slang terminology referring to the CO_2 absorbent canister.

Stack time – A term used to describe the predicted time that a canister of CO_2 absorbent will last before it needs to be replaced.

Stalactite – A speleothem that hangs from the ceiling of a cave

Stalagmite – A speleothem that grows from the floor of a cave

Static lung load (SLL; hydrostatic imbalance) – the pressure gradient between the outside and inside of the chest imposed by underwater breathing apparatus. Comfort and performance can be adversely affected, especially during exertion. The lungs can be thought of as having a center (lung centroid) located approximately 17 cm below and 7 cm behind the suprasternal notch on the chest. SLL represents the difference between the pressure delivered by the breathing apparatus (at the start of an inspiration) and the pressure at the lung centroid. If gas is delivered to the diver at a pressure equal to the depth of the lung centroid then no SLL is imposed. A person immersed to the neck has pressure inside the chest at atmospheric and outside the chest at the elevated water pressure. This represents negative SLL and can be measured as the depth of the lung centroid. A negative SLL will make a person breathe at smaller lung volumes, while a positive SLL makes a person breathe at larger lung volumes. For scuba diving, the placement of the regulator determines the SLL. A regulator in the mouth of an upright diver imposes a negative SLL. If the vertical diver were head down then the SLL would be positive. A prone diver may have a slightly positive SLL. A diver swimming shoulder down will not have an SLL imposed. With rebreathers, the placement of rebreathing bags and the amount of gas therein determines SLL. Since gas collects at the top of the bags, the orientation of the diver also matters. The depth of the bottom of the gas bubble determines the pressure delivered by the breathing apparatus. The SLL is then equal to the difference between this pressure and the pressure at the lung centroid. A backmounted bag will impose a negative SLL. A chest-mounted bag will impose a positive SLL. Over-the-shoulder bags with the right amount of gas in them may have a neutral SLL, but the actual SLL varies with gas volume and can be positive or negative. If a diver with an over-the-shoulder bag rebreather swims with a shoulder down then the SLL may be negative since the gas will collect in the upper bag; should the gas volume be large enough that all breathing is in the lower bag then the SLL will be positive. Should the gas volume in the upper bag be such that an exhalation forces some gas into the lower bag, then a sudden large pressure increase is required by the respiratory muscles.

Statistical dependence – a condition in which two variables are not independent.

Stygobites - Aquatic troglobites.

Sump – A water-filled section of a cave that terminates an air-filled passage of a cave.

Sump diving – A type of cave diving that marries dry caving, or spelunking, with cave diving.

T

Tannic water – Reddish colored water, which is stained by leachate from particular trees.

Technical diving – A form of scuba diving that exceeds conventional limits, generally including dives that are deeper than 130 ft (40 m), using mixed gas, requiring multiple cylinders or decompression, or taking place within overhead environments.

Temperature stick – An array of thermal sensors aligned in the scrubber canister to monitor the thermal activity of the scrubber (measuring the advance of the thermal front) to provide information on scrubber depletion. Also known to as a Temstick or Thermal profile monitor (TPM).

Traverse – A cave dive that takes a diver on a course from one opening to another.

Trimix – A gas mixture containing three constituents; usually oxygen, nitrogen, and helium.

Troglobites – A species that is uniquely adapted to caves and lives out its entire life cycle in caves.

Troglophiles – A species that may complete a life cycle in caves but are also widely known outside of caves.

Trogloxene – A species that uses caves, but cannot complete their life cycle entirely in caves.

Trust-me dive – A dive where a buddy surrenders their ability to self-rescue or buddy-rescue after placing trust in a diving partner to lead them safely through a dive that is beyond their experience to conduct independently.

U

Underground lake – A large lake within an air-filled cave passage.

Upstream – A relative direction with respect to the flow of gas through the breathing loop of a rebreather; the opposite of downstream.

or

Swimming into the current or outflow of a cave.

Upstream check-valve – A one-way valve system that permits inhaled gas to flow from the inhalation breathing hose to the mouthpiece, but prevents exhaled gas from flowing backwards. This valve is part of the breathing loop system that enables circular flow of gas.

V

Vadose – Refers to cave passages or spaces that are formed above the water table.

Venting breath – A type of breathing pattern used to purge gas from a breathing loop; accomplished by inhaling through the mouth and exhaling through the nose into the mask or around the edge of the mouthpiece, thus creating bubbles.

Volume-averaged pressure (aka resistive effort) – Terminology used by US Navy Experimental Diving Unit (NEDU) to describe work of breathing (WOB) in correct physical units and physiological terms. It is equivalent to the difference between inhalation and exhalation pressures averaged across a diver's breath, and is sensitive to flow resistance.

Voting algorithm/logic – the procedure in which rebreather electronics rely upon output from multiple sensors to determine when oxygen needs to be added and when sensors are faulty and signals need to be ignored. This approach assumes statistical independence of sensors, which may not be valid since the sensors are exposed to the same conditions for part of their history, possibly all of it if they are from the same manufacturing lot, and they are monitored by the same measurement system.

W

Whole-body oxygen toxicity – See pulmonary oxygen toxicity.

Work of breathing (WOB) – The effort required to complete an inspiration and expiration cycle of breathing. For a breathing apparatus, the work of breathing can be affected by breathing hose diameters, check valve design, scrubber design, depth, absorbent material, and other factors. The placement of counterlungs does not affect the WOB, but is a respiratory load by itself.

Workload – A representation of the level of physical exertion; often measured through oxygen consumption in a laboratory setting.